How to Start and Run a
Home Tutoring
Business

How to Start and Run a
Home Tutoring Business

**A complete manual for setting up
and running your own tutoring agency**

Gillian Stellman and Vivienne Howse

howtobooks

Published by How To Books Ltd,
Spring Hill House, Spring Hill Road,
Begbroke, Oxford OX5 1RX, United Kingdom
Tel: (01865) 375794. Fax: (01865) 379162
info@howtobooks.co.uk
www.howtobooks.co.uk

British Library Cataloguing in Publication Data.
A catalogue record for this book is available from the British Library.

ISBN: 978 1 84528 178 6

Produced for How To Books by Deer Park Productions, Tavistock, Devon
Typeset by PDQ Typesetting, Newcastle-under-Lyme, Staffordshire
Printed and bound in Great Britain by Bell & Bain Ltd, Scotland

NOTE: The material contained in this book is set out in good faith for general
guidance and no liability can be accepted for loss or expense incurred as a result of
relying in particular circumstances on statements made in the book. Laws and
regulations are complex and liable to change, and readers should check the current
position with the relevant authorities before making personal arrangements.

Contents

List of Figures

Preface

'They always say time changes things, but you actually have to change them yourself.'

ANDY WARHOL

You are standing in the bookshop with this manual in your hand. You are going back to your job in an office, a school or a shop after a holiday and you just can't face it. You don't like your boss, your head teacher or your manager, and you are fed up with the journey to work, the long hours and being told what to do. You are not sure what you want to do, but you do know that you want a change of lifestyle.

You have picked up the very book that is going to help you achieve this.

The aim of this publication is to encourage and enthuse people who are seeking a flexible lifestyle, which will allow them greater freedom while still earning a living. If you are one of those people who have not had the courage to take the first step towards a better way of life, this book is that first step. Buy this book now so that you can change your lifestyle when the time is right for you.

Starting a new business venture can be disconcerting if you have not been in business before. Our manual, built up over many years of our own experience, is highly practical and should reassure you that no aspect of the business is half understood or half explained. It eliminates the trial-and-error period, the money wasted on unworkable ideas and puts you straight onto the first step of a successful business career.

While most books are general guides, this is a straightforward and easy-to-follow manual covering every aspect from how to begin to how to achieve success running your own tutoring agency. You could, in fact, buy this book on Friday, read it over the weekend and start your own business on Monday. Its unique, proven successful formula combines the blueprint for a flourishing business with an individual and caring service. It is a rare find.

Part I
THE MANUAL

1

WHY A TUTORING AGENCY?

*'Education is the most powerful weapon
which you can use to change the world.'*

NELSON MANDELA

There are many reasons why a tutoring agency is an excellent choice of business venture and has a wide appeal.

EDUCATION IS ALWAYS TOPICAL

Education is a constant in our lives. Every parent worries about their child's education and there is an ever increasing need for better qualifications in a highly competitive world. More and more parents are turning to professional tutoring agents to find the help needed for their children in an education system that does not always provide enough support for children's differing needs. A tutoring agency provides a valuable and much-appreciated service.

AN INTERESTING BUSINESS

You will find that running a tutoring agency is fun, exciting and that every day is different. During the course of any one day you may be dealing with tutors, clients, advertising departments, accountants or schools. It is very satisfying when your advertising campaign has exceeded expectation and you have recruited excellent new tutors, when the business is busy and you are taking lots of bookings, and when tuition has been successful and you get positive feedback from clients. You have the opportunity to help a wide range of people: the A-level student needing reassurance, the worried parent whose child has had a poor end of term report and the new tutors who need the confidence you will give them to take on their first client.

BEING YOUR OWN BOSS

You have reached the stage in your life when you want to be your own boss and make choices about the way in which you work. Choosing to start your own tutoring agency will radically alter and enhance your lifestyle because you can make it fit around family or other work commitments, leisure pursuits and holidays. Whether you choose to run your agency full time or part time, your working timetable will be flexible. You have complete control over when you do your work. For example, you may do a little paperwork each evening, or you may prefer to do it all in one go once a week. You will not be committed to sitting by the telephone all day because a good answering system will ensure that you do not miss any calls from clients or tutors. Your business is portable. Even when you are away from home you may wish to take the business with you. You can do this by transferring calls to your mobile or to a local landline and by taking with you a laptop or the subjects list (see Chapter 3, Figure 11). On a sunny day you can work from the bottom of your garden!

WORKING FROM HOME

You will find that setting up your tutoring agency in your own home saves you the time and energy of looking for business premises. It also frees you from the huge financial burden of buying or renting a property, paying business rates, utility bills, solicitors' fees and purchasing furniture and equipment for these premises. In fact, the only initial outlay is the cost of your advertising.

In addition, a fair proportion of the total overheads of your home (telephone bill, heating bill, wear and tear) can be offset against your tax bill. The fact that you are running your business from home will not affect your community charge bill as long as no room in your home is used purely for business purposes.

A GOOD INCOME

You can make a good income from your tutoring business. It is one of the very few businesses in which there will be an immediate financial return. If you start your agency on 1 May, money will start coming in by 1 June. Realistically, any business takes one year to become well established and to build a good reputation. You may decide from the outset to put all your energy into setting up your business, making it your sole source of income. Alternatively, you can run it alongside your existing job as a second income.

NO TRAINING REQUIRED

You can do it! This is not a business for which you need vast amounts of training. It is a business which is suitable for anyone who is interested in education and is familiar with the education system. You will need a sense of humour, patience, good organisational and communication skills and the ability to deal sensitively with the public. You can run the agency on your own or with a business partner.

WHAT'S IN A NAME?

Now you have decided that a tutoring agency is exactly what you are looking for, you need to choose a name for your business. Take your time over this, because it will be too costly to change once your advertising campaign is underway and your stationery is printed. A good name, short and memorable, must tell clients what sort of business you are. Bear in mind that you are an educational enterprise and while a gimmicky name such as 'Education is us', or 'Teach'm rite' might seem fun, this would not be in keeping with the image you wish to project.

THE RIGHT CATCHMENT AREA

You need to give careful consideration to the catchment area which your tutoring agency will serve.

You do not need to limit this to the precise area in which you live. If you live in a quiet rural area, you can set up your agency to operate in the nearest large town. Do not be too ambitious initially with the size of area you choose, you can always extend it later when you have more experience. Ideally, your agency should service a densely populated area where there are many primary and secondary schools.

Once you have selected your area, familiarise yourself with the local schools. It will be useful for you to know the names of all the schools in the area, their size, entrance requirements and their academic level. This information is easily accessible from the local education authority website or at any local library.

It would be useful to know the local geographical area in which you are operating your agency and a good local map will provide this information. This is needed when matching pupils to tutors so that you do not ask either party to travel unreasonable distances to lessons.

IN SUMMARY

A tutoring agency is an exciting and rewarding business, and with the guidance of this manual you will take the first step towards a new and successful career.

2

WHERE DO I BEGIN?

*'Where shall I begin, please your Majesty?'
the White Rabbit asked. 'Begin at the
beginning,' the King said gravely, 'and go
on till you come to the end: then stop.'*

LEWIS CARROLL

The very beginning of a home tutoring business is the recruitment of
tutors.

In this manual the definition of a tutor is: a current teacher, retired
teacher, a teacher taking time out or a graduate with some teaching
experience. Key to making a success of your business is recruiting a
sufficient number of good tutors.

Figure 1 shows a basic recruitment advertisement:

TEACHERS AND EXPERIENCED TUTORS
Required immediately by busy tutoring agency
020 8666 4222
any time

Fig. 1. Recruitment advert 1.

You need to do this because you cannot advertise for clients until you
can provide them with an appropriate tutor. In order to get your
business off the ground you need to initiate an efficient, dynamic
recruitment campaign. You will mainly recruit tutors from advertising.
However, you may already know tutors through work contacts and
friends who wish to join your agency. This is known as networking. You

may wonder why tutors are keen to join your agency when they can advertise for clients for themselves and not have to pay commission to you.

WHY TUTORS REGISTER

There are two main reasons why tutors will register with your agency. Firstly, advertising is expensive. A weekly advert is necessary in order to keep a constant flow of pupils and this is done for them by the agency. Secondly, all fees are set for tutors by the agency (see Chapters 3 and 8 for details of fees, pp. 19 and 51). Great consideration has gone into setting prices which strike the balance between making it a worthwhile job for tutors and at the same time affordable for clients (See Chapters 3 and 8, pp. 19 and 51). This releases tutors from the responsibility of negotiating fees individually with their clients.

WHEN TO ADVERTISE

Initial recruitment

This should be carried out for a period of six consecutive weeks before advertising for clients. This allows sufficient time for the advertisement to be seen by enough tutors for you to recruit the required numbers.

You may feel overwhelmed by the response to your advertisement but you need large numbers of tutors especially in the key subject areas of GCSE Maths and Science and all Primary subjects.

Ongoing recruitment

This is needed to boost the number of tutors required as more clients apply to your agency. Timing is of the essence as recruitment adverts are costly. For example, don't waste money advertising at the end of a term when teachers are likely to be exhausted and in need of a break.

The most cost-effective way of recruitment advertising is to place the advert at a time when tutors are more likely to respond to the advert and when the demand for tutors by clients is at its peak. The times which have proven to be the most successful are:

Mid-September
- At the start of a new academic year tutors are fresh and enthusiastic.
- Parents begin to think ahead to secondary school transfer and possible entrance exams.
- Pupils begin to realise that their GCSEs and A-levels are on the horizon.
- Younger children may need help adjusting to the greater demands of their new class.

The beginning of November
- With the approach of Christmas, tutors look for an opportunity to earn extra money.
- Parents' and pupils' minds turn to entrance examinations and course-work, and they may request extra tuition in the school holidays.

The end of January
- Exam pressure is mounting and the demand for tutoring is great.

Four weeks before Easter
- Primary-level tutors are available to take on new pupils as their existing pupils have completed their entrance examinations.
- Senior school teachers have seen their GCSE and A-level students complete their courses and they have more time to take on tutoring.
- Pupils seek last-minute help with exam preparation at all levels.

SPECIFIC SUBJECT RECRUITMENT

During the academic year you may need to use your advertisement to target tutors in specific subjects in order to meet an immediate demand. You can use the same basic recruitment advert but highlight the specific subject as shown in Figure 2 below:

> TEACHERS AND EXPERIENCED TUTORS
> Required immediately in all subjects especially
> Maths, Science and Primary
> 020 8666 4222
> any time

Figure 2. Recruitment advert 2.

In addition you should:

♦ Make use of personal contacts who may have friends or colleagues who teach the required subject.

♦ Contact tutors who are registered with you and who are currently teaching at a school to ask them if a colleague in the appropriate subject is interested in tutoring.

♦ This is an excellent opportunity for you to make contact with tutors who you have not used for some time to see if they are still available.

♦ Check your local paper for tutors advertising independently who teach the required subject and contact them to ask if they would like to register with your agency.

♦ When corresponding with schools, tutors and referees always enclose one or two recruitment leaflets (see Figure 5, p. 14) with a polite note asking them to draw this to the attention of anyone who might be interested.

WHERE TO ADVERTISE

For people looking for tutoring work, the local newspaper is likely to be their first port of call. This will have a dedicated education recruitment section. If there is more than one local newspaper don't necessarily choose the one with the largest circulation; choose the one that is known to have the best recruitment section.

Your local paper will prove to be an invaluable means of recruiting tutors at a reasonable price. Since you will be advertising for six continuous weeks initially and then regularly throughout the year, negotiate a good rate with the advertising team. Establish a good working rapport with that team as this will be useful to your advertising campaign. As a guideline, the cost of a 3×1cm box recruitment advertisement is approximately £85 plus VAT.

Send a carefully worded letter which introduces your services to the head teachers of local schools, at the same time mentioning that you are recruiting tutors. As a follow-up (see Figure 3) at a later date send a second letter to the head teachers enclosing recruitment leaflets (see Figure 4). Politely request that leaflets are placed on staff noticeboards or handed to their staff. Target 20 different schools per term so that you do not inundate the same schools with your literature every term.

Be selective

Just as the timing of your advert is crucial, the choice of where to advertise is equally important. Do not be tempted to place your advertisement in every possible publication in order to attract new tutors. Target publications with a clearly defined education section, where your advert will be seen in context. You may think that magazines produced by schools, churches or the local fête committee would be the ideal place to advertise. However, this is not where teachers or tutors will be looking for work.

The following points will also help your recruitment campaign:

- Laminate the same leaflet and place it on the noticeboard of libraries in your area for a period of 4–8 weeks. The cost of this is minimal. This is particularly effective during school holidays when teachers may be looking for extra work.

- Have business cards produced. These need not be elaborate or glossy. A simple, clearly worded card is just as effective and less expensive to produce. Remember to carry them with you at all times so that you can take every opportunity to recruit new tutors.

EDGSTONE TUTORS
69 High Road, Edgstone, London E12 9SZ
Telephone 020 8666 4222

FOR THE ATTENTION OF THE HEAD TEACHER

Dear Sir/Madam

I would like to introduce my agency to you and would very much welcome the opportunity to meet you.

The agency offers individual lessons in all subjects, at all levels, tailor-made revision courses and remedial tuition, carefully matching pupils to tutors. I am especially keen to offer extra help to children at your recommendation and the tutors would be happy to ensure that their work complemented and supported your curriculum.

I would be happy to talk to members of staff who would like to know more about the agency with a view to recommending pupils or who may have time to do some tutoring themselves.

I look forward to hearing from you.

Yours faithfully

For Edgstone Tutors

Fig. 3. Letter 1: For the attention of the head teacher.

EDGSTONE TUTORS
69 High Road, Edgstone, London E12 9SZ
Telephone 020 8666 4222

FOR THE ATTENTION OF THE HEAD TEACHER

Dear Sir/Madam

We would be grateful if you would consider placing one of our leaflets
on your staff noticeboard and passing some on to members of your
teaching staff who may be interested in tutoring in their spare time.
This may be of particular interest to your part-time or supply teachers.

Yours faithfully

For Edgstone Tutors

Enc.

Fig. 4. Letter 2: For the attention of the head teacher.

WOULD YOU LIKE TO EARN EXTRA CASH IN YOUR SPARE TIME?

TEACHERS AND
EXPERIENCED TUTORS

NEEDED BY BUSY TUTORING AGENCY TO TUTOR CHILDREN IN ALL SUBJECTS FROM PRIMARY TO A-LEVEL

**FOR MORE DETAILS AND AN APPLICATION
FORM PLEASE TELEPHONE**

020 8666 4222

At any time

Fig. 5. 'Would you like to earn extra cash in your spare time?' leaflet.

◆ Networking is an effective way to use all your personal contacts to advertise the fact that you are looking for new tutors.

◆ Tutors who advertise their services in the local papers may also be happy to work for you. It is worth a telephone call to check this possibility.

◆ Even when advertising for clients always include the words 'New tutors welcome' in the advertisement.

◆ The *Times Educational Supplement* is an expensive paper in which to advertise but does specifically target teachers. However, it is a nationally distributed paper and should you decide to advertise there, you need to specify in the advertisement the geographical areas in which tutors are required.

MONITORING YOUR ADVERT

You need to check your advert every week in order to make sure that you are getting value for money.

◆ First of all, make sure that the advert actually appears in the newspaper!

◆ Never pay for an advert which is even slightly incorrect. A whole week of advertising can be wasted if the newspaper gets it wrong, for example if they omit your telephone number. Should this happen, negotiate at least one free week of advertising.

◆ Ask for a proof copy of the advert when changing the wording. This can be done easily and quickly by either fax or email.

◆ The best position on the page for an advertisement is at eye level. Whilst the advertising team can never guarantee this position for your advert every week, complain to them if it is constantly placed at the bottom of the page, where it is difficult to spot, or in the fold of the newspaper, where it is difficult to read.

Once you have established a good working rapport with the sales staff at the newspaper office they will be much more inclined to deal sympathetically with any complaints or problems you may have. The expertise of friendly advertising staff can be of enormous benefit to any business.

IN SUMMARY

The three Rs rule applies – the right wording, the right time, the right place. These are essential to a successful recruitment advertising campaign.

The right wording

Select the wording for your advertisement carefully. Have a basic advert to which you can make additions or adjustments when necessary. For example, if you particularly need to recruit Science teachers add a simple sentence to your basic advertisement. Do not be tempted to overcrowd the advertisement; it will not look good and will be difficult to read.

If you need to say more, book a slightly larger box. It is well worth the small extra cost.

The right time

Time your advert to appear when teachers are likely to be seeking extra money or when they have the least work. Make a note in your business diary of the dates on which your advert appears and note the response to it. This will enable you to get the timing right each year for your ongoing recruitment.

The right place

Choose your local paper carefully. This should be the one which is widely read in the areas where you want to operate your agency and which has an excellent education recruitment section. Ignore advertising sales people who offer to put your business name on promotional items such as pens or who wish to sell you a car registration number plate with your business initials on it!

3

WHAT HAPPENS NEXT?

'Teachers affect eternity; they can never tell where their influence stops.'

HENRY B. ADAMS

DEALING WITH THE RESPONSE TO YOUR RECRUITMENT CAMPAIGN

When potential tutors ring in response to your advertisement, the initial information you will need from them is their name, address, telephone number and the subjects they want to teach. At this stage, this is all the information you need, because you will be sending them a comprehensive information for tutors application form, which will elicit much more detailed information (see Figure 6). Keep a list of all enquiries.

Enquirers may want to ask you lots of questions about the agency but you can keep verbal information to a minimum by explaining that you will be sending a clear and concise information for tutors form which has been designed to give tutors all the information they need before registering with your agency (see Figure 7). They may also suggest a meeting but it is too big a task and too time consuming to interview prospective tutors.

You do need to speak to the person who wishes to tutor and not to someone ringing on their behalf. Even the briefest time spent talking to a potential tutor will give you an idea of whether they will be suitable for your agency. Use your instincts. For example, if you cannot clearly understand what the prospective tutor is saying on the telephone, it is unlikely that they will be able to communicate easily with pupils, or you may feel that the tutor is far too inexperienced. Do not be afraid to turn tutors away.

EDGSTONE TUTORS
69 High Road, Edgstone, London E12 9SZ
Telephone 020 8666 4222

APPLICATION FORM

Name: ....

Address:...

....

Telephone: .... Date of birth: ....

Email:..

Please give full details of the **subjects** and **levels** you are able to teach:

Subjects	Levels
1.	PRIMARY GCSE A-LEVEL
2.	PRIMARY GCSE A-LEVEL
3.	PRIMARY GCSE A-LEVEL

Any additional subjects/levels: ....

NB. It is essential that GCSE and A-level tutors are familiar with current exam requirements and have up-to-date syllabuses and papers.

Details of teaching experience:

Please give details of days/times you are available to teach, e.g. mornings, afternoons, evenings, weekends:

Would you prefer to teach in your own home or would you be prepared to travel to pupils' homes?

Do you have your own transport?

PLEASE ENCLOSE AN UP-TO-DATE CV AND THE NAMES AND ADDRESSES OF TWO REFEREES IN THE UK WITH THIS APPLICATION FORM.

Declaration: Information given in this application is true and complete. I agree to abide by the terms and conditions specified on the enclosed information sheet.

TAX AND NATIONAL INSURANCE

I understand that as a tutor I am regarded as self-employed and responsible for my own contributions.

Signed.................................. Date ....

Encs. (information sheet)

Fig. 6. Application form.

EDGSTONE TUTORS
69 High Road, Edgstone, London E12 9SZ
Telephone 020 8666 4222
INFORMATION FOR TUTORS FORM

FEES AND COMMISSIONS

	Primary	GCSE level	A-level	Special needs	Higher levels
Cost of lesson	£20	£22	£24	£24	£25
Tutor's fee	£17	£19	£21	£21	£22
Agency commission	£3	£3	£3	£3	£3

For students sharing lessons: First student pays full amount, those sharing pay half. The total fee is then divided equally amongst the students so that each one benefits from a discount.

An administration fee of £5 is charged to each client by the agency.

◆ Tutors are paid by the client at the end of each lesson.
◆ Tutors collect the administration fee on the agency's behalf at the end of the first lesson.
◆ Tutors may charge up to £2 for travelling expenses.
◆ Tutors must inform the agency of any clients obtained by contacts originally made through Edgstone Tutoring Agency.
◆ Tutors must agree to pay the set commission for clients introduced through Edgstone Tutoring Agency.

It is essential that GCSE and A-level tutors are familiar with current exam requirements and have up-to-date syllabuses and papers.

CANCELLATIONS
◆ Make a note of your client's telephone number in case you have to contact him/her.
◆ 24 hours' notice of cancellation is required of both tutor and client.
◆ If the required notice is not given you are entitled, at your discretion, to charge a cancellation fee.

PROCEDURES
◆ When the agency receives calls from prospective clients we will contact a suitable tutor.
◆ Tutors should then call the client immediately or as soon as possible to arrange a convenient time to commence lessons.
◆ Tutors should inform the agency immediately of the arrangements made/outcome of the call.
◆ Tutors should keep a record of all lessons taught on the timesheet provided.
◆ Timesheets must be completed by tutors and signed by the client at the end of each lesson.
◆ At the end of each month timesheets, commission and administration fees should be sent to the agency.

TAX AND NATIONAL INSURANCE
All tutors are regarded as self-employed and responsible for their own contributions.

Fig. 7. Information for tutors form.

MEETING THE CRITERIA

Do not waste time and money sending information to applicants unless they meet the following criteria:

◆ They live within the catchment area of your agency. Do not be persuaded by someone who lives a long way off but insists that they are happy to travel any distance. In reality, this would not be financially worth their while for a one-hour lesson, and on a dark and icy winter's evening they will feel less inclined to make that journey.

◆ They have appropriate qualifications in the subjects they want to teach. Parents will expect tutors to have a suitable level of expertise in the subjects they are teaching. This will mean that the tutors have a degree or a teaching qualification. However pleasant or persuasive a 17-year-old A-level student might be, they would be unacceptable to parents as a tutor.

◆ They know the national curriculum, examination system, local school entrance requirements and standards required by examination boards at the level they are going to teach. They will need to be prepared to furnish themselves with resources such as course books and examination papers.

◆ They are available to teach at times convenient to school-age children. It is not worth your while taking on a tutor who is only available evenings after 9.30 p.m.

◆ They intend to stay in your catchment area for some considerable time as it is disruptive for pupils to have to change tutors.

◆ They teach national curriculum subjects. You may have an applicant who is qualified to teach Manchurian Chinese but it is highly unlikely that there will be a demand for such specialist subjects.

When sending the application form and information for tutors form you need to enclose a disclaimer form (see Figure 8).

All of these forms could be sent by email, thus avoiding the cost and delay of postage. However, they do need to be returned to you by post because both the application form and the disclaimer form need to be signed by the tutor.

EDGSTONE TUTORS
69 High Street, Edgstone, London E12 9SZ
020 8666 4222

DISCLAIMER FORM

ALL PROSPECTIVE TUTORS MUST COMPLETE AND SIGN THIS FORM.

Have you ever been investigated by a Social Services Department as being an actual or potential risk to children or young people? **YES/NO**

If YES, please supply details: ....

....

IMPORTANT
I understand that this work will involve access to children and young people, and I hereby consent to Edgstone Tutors checking my information with the Criminal Records Bureau (CRB) and/or the Police and/or Social Services.

Signed:.................................... Date:................................

Please also print your name..

If you are currently teaching in a school and have already been CRB checked, please enclose a copy of the CRB disclosure.

Fig. 8. Disclaimer form.

CHASING UP APPLICATIONS

Once you have sent the necessary forms, allow two to three weeks for a reply. If after this period you have had no response, contact the tutor to encourage them to send in their application form. This is particularly valuable for the large numbers of tutors that you need in key subject areas. A small percentage of applicants never respond. You can contact tutors by telephone or by sending a reminder slip (See Figure 9).

EDGSTONE TUTORS
69 High Street, Edgstone, London E12 9SZ
020 8666 4222

We sent an application form to you some time ago and you have not yet returned it to us. We are very keen to recruit people with your expertise and would like to encourage you to complete and return the form. If you did not receive the form or you have mislaid it, please phone us and we will send you another one.

Fig. 9. Reminder slip.

REFERENCES

As stated on the application form all tutors must provide the names and addresses of two referees residing in this country. Either academic or character references are acceptable. A reference letter should be sent to both referees (see Figure 10).

A pro-forma reference letter makes providing a reference so simple for the referee that you should get an excellent response rate to your requests without having to go to the expense of sending a stamped, addressed envelope.

It is essential to obtain two references for each tutor. You may need to contact the new tutor if you do not receive their references and ask them to encourage their referees to respond.

Should you need to use a new tutor urgently before receiving their

EDGSTONE TUTORS
69 High Road, Edgstone, London E12 9SZ
Telephone 020 8666 4222

Date ....

Dear

Re ....

The above named has applied to this agency to tutor children on a one-to-one basis or in small groups in the subject(s) of

....

Your name was given as a referee and we would be most grateful if you could complete the following brief questionnaire and return the whole letter to us as soon as possible. Any information provided will be treated in strict confidence. Thank you for your help.

.... For Edgstone Tutors

In what capacity do you know the above named

     EMPLOYER/FRIEND/COLLEAGUE/OTHER (please specify).

How long have you known him/her?

Is there any reason why you would not consider him/her suitable for this type of work?

Please add any other comments/recommendations which you consider relevant if you have any:

Signed ....

Date ....

Fig. 10. Reference letter.

written references, you could ask the tutor to provide you with a telephone number for at least one of their referees, who could then give you an instant reference.

VETTING

You can use the Criminal Records Bureau (CRB) to vet your prospective tutors. The CRB can provide either an enhanced or a standard disclosure. An enhanced disclosure will inform you of any criminal record incurred by the person you are vetting. A standard disclosure will inform you if that person has ever been banned from working with children. The cost of an enhanced disclosure is £36 and a standard disclosure £31. However, you cannot access this information directly if you are a small organisation, i.e. if you are making less than 2,000 enquiries per year. If this is the case you can use an umbrella body to get the information, but this will incur an additional cost to those charged by the CRB. There is a list of umbrella bodies on the CRB website.

Many tutors will already have a CRB disclosure obtained by their employers before they began working with children. The disclaimer form which you send with the application form and the information for tutors form ask for a copy of this.

You need to think very carefully before committing your agency to obtaining a CRB disclosure for every tutor given the high cost of this procedure and the length of time it takes. All the information you need about the CRB is available at www.crb.gov.uk or telephone 0870 909 0811.

PARENTAL RESPONSIBILITY

Ultimately, parents are responsible for their children's safety. The client information form, which you send to parents confirming the booking (see Chapter 6, Figure 22), clearly states that 'the agency cannot under any circumstances be held responsible for the acts or omissions of the tutor introduced or for any loss, expense or damage incurred'.

MANUAL RECORD KEEPING

Once you have received a completed and signed application form, disclaimer form and two references you need to put the tutors' information into a tutors' card index system.

You also need to start a subjects list, which groups tutors together under the subjects they teach and the level at which they teach them. All you need to put on the list is the tutor's name, geographical area or postcode, telephone number and whether they are a teacher (Te), tutor (Tu) or student (Stu) (see Figure 11).

COMPUTERISED RECORD KEEPING

If you are keeping computerised records, you need to add the tutors' information to your database. Figure 12 shows a blank record, Figure 13 shows a completed record.

If you are using computerised record keeping, a printed copy of the subjects list is not strictly necessary but could be useful as a back-up in the event of computer failure or if for a period of time you do not have access to a computer. To compile a subjects list, simply copy the 'Sub list info' field in your database into a subjects list file and print it.

The information stored on your agency database does not contravene the Data Protection Act. This is because you are not storing sensitive information on tutors, such as their physical or mental health status, nor are you passing on any information about tutors to a third party.

SUBJECTS LIST

CHEMISTRY A-LEVEL

BAKER Sarita E20 8669 3902 Tu
CARTER Julia E12 8666 7890 Tu
DeSANTOS Jessica E12 8666 3725 Tu
FLEMING Joseph E20 8669 6951 Tu
KAMDEN Bulka E20 07913 428851 Tu
LAW Rabinder E10 8667 1325 Stu
MCCOUGH Martin E20 8669 6632 Te
OLIVER John E12 8666 8523 Te
REDMAN Zorah (Dr) E10 8667 0734 Te
SPENCER Suresh E20 8669 9982 Te
VICTOR Susan E12 07792 877063 Te
WINSTON Padma E12 8666 7354 Te

CHEMISTRY GCSE

AUSTIN Isaac E12 8666 4989 Te
BRAMLEY Hugh E10 8667 1160 Te
CLARK Jane E10 8667 4888 Tu
DEARING Bernadette E10 8667 4857 Te
DACRES Rumana E20 8669 4551 Tu
JAGAN Wajiha E12 8666 6925 Te
KULKARNI Savindra E10 8667 1097 Tu
LISTER Melvyn E12 8666 8199 Te
MARTIN Lisa E10 8667 8717 Tu
SIMCA Arshad E10 8667 5838 Tu
SHAH Aerim E20 86691186 Te
WALTERS Omowunmi E10 05540474495 Tu
VALENTINO Rudo E20 8669 Te

Fig. 11. Subjects list.

THE TUTOR DATABASE (Sample 1)

Name:	Subject 1:
Address 1:	Subject 2:
Address 2:	Subject 3:
Address 3:	Subject 4:
Postcode:	Subject 5:
Tel No:	Level:
Sub list info:	Teacher/Tutor:
email:	
Date of registration:	

Subject All:

MISC INFO:
CURRENT PUPILS:
PAST PUPILS:

Fig. 12. The tutor database (Sample 1).

THE TUTOR DATABASE (Sample 2)

Name:	SMITH John	Subject 1: CHEMISTRY A
Address 1:	2 Green Street	Subject 2: BIOLOGY GCSE
Address 2:	Edgstone	Subject 3:
Address 3:	London	Subject 4:
Postcode:	E12 2ZX	Subject 5:
Tel No:	020 8666 4567	Level: GCSE/A
Sub list info:	E12 8666 4567 Te	Teacher/Tutor: Teacher
email:	jsmith@hotmail.com	
Date of registration:	06.06.05	

Subject All: CHEMISTRY, BIOLOGY

MISC INFO: d.o.b. 4.4.72 (m) 07777 123456
CURRENT PUPILS: Jackson 04/06/06 Greening 30/06/06
PAST PUPILS: Phelps 27/06/05, Mills 14/09/05, Jenkins 17/10/05

Fig. 13. The tutor database (Sample 2).

4

GETTING YOUR BUSINESS GOING

'An advertisement must offer a promise to the reader of a believable benefit and it must be phrased in a way to make it memorable.'

MORRIS HITE

ADVERTISING FOR CLIENTS

What to advertise

Use a simple, basic advert containing your agency name, telephone number and a catchy slogan. 'Matching pupils to tutors from Primary to A-level' is an excellent slogan which encapsulates the essence of your tutoring business. Although you are now advertising for clients, never miss the opportunity to attract more tutors. This can be done by adding the three simple words 'New tutors welcome' at the bottom of every advertisement.

EDGSTONE TUTORS

Matching pupils to tutors from Primary to A-level

020 8666 4222
any time

New tutors welcome

Fig. 14. Advert for clients 1.

This basic advert can be adapted at appropriate times throughout the year. For example, in the lead-up to summer holidays, your agency may offer short language courses.

EDGSTONE TUTORS

Short language courses available

Matching pupils to tutors from Primary to A-level

020 8666 4222

any time

New tutors welcome

Fig. 15. Advert for clients 2.

Where to advertise

Your weekly advertisement for clients should be put into the education section of the most widely read local newspaper. Select the paper that you and your neighbours would use when seeking a local service. The cost of a 3 × 1cm advertisement will be approximately £40 per week. Negotiate the best possible price with the advertising sales team. Discounts should be available for long-term continuous advertising.

Check your advertisement every week to make sure that it actually appears, that the wording and spelling are correct and that it is in a good position on the page. When making any changes to your advertisement always ask for a proof copy to see how it looks and to check that it is correct. Do not pay if the advertisement is incorrect. Whilst you will not be guaranteed the best position for your advertisement every week, make sure that it is not consistently badly placed.

You may wish to have your own website. Whilst the expense of creating a website might seem a little daunting, the cost of running it is minimal. The internet is thought of as a worldwide medium and you may feel that it would not be useful for a business covering a relatively small geographical area. However, more and more people seeking a local service will find it via Google and other search engines on the internet. You can set up a website yourself or use a web designer to do it for you. If you are keen to do this yourself but lack the necessary skills, you can avail yourself of the many publications on the subject or use the internet.

You could also deliver leaflets door to door (see Figure 16), and leave leaflets in places which are frequented by families, for example tennis clubs, swimming clubs, dentists and nurseries.

Local libraries also have large noticeboards advertising a range of activities, events and services. This is a cheap and effective way of advertising which you can use all year round or intermittently to boost your business.

Make use of all your personal contacts. The more people who know that your agency is up and running, the better. Always carry business cards with you so that you can give them to anyone who you think may be interested and they in turn can pass them on to others.

Once your advertisement appears regularly, other local newspapers will try to persuade you to advertise with them. Having selected the most appropriate newspaper in which to advertise your business, additional advertising in another newspaper would be an unnecessary expense. Church magazines, school fête programmes and other similar publications may well reach parents with children but this is not where parents will look for a tutor for their children.

When to advertise

- ◆ You need to advertise for clients every week in your local paper.

- ◆ At the beginning of each term target ten schools with an introduction letter (see Chapter 2, Letter 1). Choose different schools each time.

- ◆ Once a term target one or two specific geographical areas with a leaflet drop (see Figure 16).

```
EDGSTONE TUTORS

HAS TEACHERS AVAILABLE TO TUTOR CHILDREN AT
ALL LEVELS IN ALL SUBJECTS


For more information call
020 8666 4222


ADDITIONAL TEACHERS ALWAYS NEEDED
```

Fig. 16. Leaflet.

If you do not wish to distribute leaflets yourself nor pay professional leafleteers, enlist the help of friends' children, the local Boy Scouts or similar organisations. A payment of £5 per hour is appropriate and you could expect them to deliver approximately 250 leaflets per hour. You need to give written instructions to leafleteers (see Figure 17) plus a map highlighting the streets they are to target.

GUIDELINES FOR LEAFLETEERS

◆ Do not deliver to properties where there is multiple occupancy (i.e. houses split into flats, blocks of flats, etc).

◆ Fold the leaflet carefully and only once.

◆ Make sure the leaflet goes right through the letterbox.

◆ Keep a record of the names of the roads to which you have delivered the leaflets.

◆ Return undelivered leaflets to the agency.

Fig. 17. Guidelines for leafleteers.

Keep a list of the areas you have leafleted on each occasion so that you cover as many areas as possible.

IMPORTANT DATES IN THE SCHOOL YEAR

At specific times of the year use your basic advertisement to highlight important dates in the school year.

In July, use your advertisement to highlight the need for tuition to prepare pupils for school entrance examinations which take place between October and January. An advertisement in July will encourage parents to think ahead and book a tutor to start either during the school holidays or at the beginning of the next school term. At this time, you will have tutors to take on new students because their current students will have completed their tuition.

Entrance exams only a few months away?

EDGSTONE TUTORS

Matching pupils to tutors from Primary to A-level

020 8666 4222
Any time

New tutors welcome

Fig. 18. Advert 1.

In October, use your advertisement to highlight SATs, GCSEs and A-level tuition. By October pupils will have settled into their new academic year and will be preparing for the examinations at the end of the school year.

SATs, GCSEs/A-levels on the horizon?

EDGSTONE TUTORS
Matching pupils to tutors from Primary to A-level

020 8666 4222
Any time

New tutors welcome

Fig. 19. Advert 2.

Two to three weeks before the Christmas and Easter school holidays, advertise the fact that holiday revision courses are available through your agency.

Holiday Revision Courses available

EDGSTONE TUTORS
Matching pupils to tutors from Primary to A-level

020 8666 4222
Any time

New tutors welcome

Fig. 20. Advert 3.

5

RESPONDING TO CLIENTS' ENQUIRIES

> '*There is only one boss, the customer. He can fire everybody in the company from the chairman down, simply by spending his money somewhere else.*'
>
> SAMUEL MOORE WALTON

BOOKINGS

You may only have a very brief telephone conversation with clients. Nevertheless, this is your opportunity to make a good impression which will encourage them to use your services. Even when the agency is busy and you have had many telephone calls that day you need to be a good listener and make each client feel that they are your most important client. Sound welcoming and enthusiastic; this will instil clients with the confidence that you will do your best for them quickly and efficiently.

WHAT YOU NEED TO ASK CLIENTS

Once your agency is busy and you are dealing with many enquiries each day, it is easy to forget to ask some essential questions. Therefore a booking form is necessary to ensure that nothing is forgotten; it is also a written record of each booking (see Figure 21). This form will also enable a partner or flatmate to take a booking for you in your absence, if necessary.

The Miscellaneous Information category on the form gives you space to make a note of any additional facts that you will find helpful in choosing the right tutor. For example, when asking for the subject and the level,

BOOKING FORM

DATE OF BOOKING . . . .

NAME/ADDRESS . . . .

NAME OF CHILD . . . .

TELEPHONE NUMBER(S) . . . .

SUBJECT/LEVEL . . . .

HOME/AWAY/EITHER . . . .

SCHOOL ATTENDED . . . .

MISCELLANEOUS INFORMATION . . . .

. . . .

. . . .

WHERE DID YOU SEE OUR ADVERT? . . . .

TUTOR ALLOCATED . . . .

DATE OF FIRST LESSON . . . .

Fig. 21. Booking form.

you will need to remember that many A-level subjects are divided into several separate areas. Maths A-level consists of pure maths, mechanics and statistics and the student may need help in only one of these areas. You should clarify exactly what the pupil needs. GCSE and A-level syllabuses vary from one examination board to another and not every tutor is familiar with every syllabus. Therefore, it is necessary to know the board. If the pupil is sitting entrance exams for a specific school at 11 + or 13 +, it will be useful for the tutor to know which school.

It will also give you space to make a note of additional information that parents may offer. For example, they may tell you that the child works better for female tutors, is at boarding school and can only have tuition on Saturdays, has been ill and missed a lot of school or that the child has special educational needs.

Asking the client where they saw your advert helps you to evaluate your advertising strategy.

WHAT YOU NEED TO TELL CLIENTS

There are certain facts that you must be sure to tell clients at the outset in order to avoid confusion at a later date:

- The hourly cost of a lesson, including tutors' travelling expenses and the agency administration fee (see Chapter 8, for explanation of administration fee), p. 53.

- The sequence of events and how the agency works: the agency will select an appropriate tutor who will then contact them directly within a day or two to organise a mutually convenient time and place for the lessons. It is important to give clients this information as agencies work in different ways. Do not commit to a certain tutor at this stage, even if someone immediately springs to mind. You may find that this tutor currently has no places for new students.

- The agency will confirm the booking in writing (see Chapter 6, Figure 22, client information form).

◆ Clients should contact the agency if there are any problems. For example, if they cannot arrange a mutually convenient time for the lesson or if, once the lessons have started, the pupil does not get on well with their tutor. This reassures clients that the agency is always happy to try again.

General questions you may be asked

◆ Advice with regard to when to start tuition for exams. Explain to clients that exam tuition usually starts three or four terms before the exam itself, with breaks for school holidays.

◆ How much tuition may be needed by a child who is very behind in their work. Suggest that the child would benefit from four or five terms of tuition and may need to continue throughout the school holidays.

◆ How many hours of tuition per week a child normally needs. You can advise clients that, on a one-to-one basis one hour of tuition per week can make an enormous difference to a child's confidence and progress. However, if a child needs a last-minute boost before exams they may require two or three one-hour lessons.

◆ Whether a six-year-old child can concentrate for a whole hour. Reassure clients that experienced tutors will take this into consideration when organising lessons.

◆ The requirements for local school entrance examinations. You need to keep up to date with this information by contacting schools or education authorities every year or two so that you can provide this information.

◆ What subjects to concentrate on for a child who is out of school. Advise clients to concentrate on the basic core subjects: Maths, English and Science.

◆ To provide a tutor in each of their child's nine GCSE subjects. Advise clients against this since it would be impossible for a child to fit in nine lessons in the evenings after full days at school. Suggest concentrating the weekly tuition on two or three subjects and possibly adding other subjects during school holidays.

Explain to clients that the experienced tutor who will be contacting them will be in a better position to give advice on all the above questions once they have had the opportunity to assess a child's needs.

Specific questions you may be asked about tutors

You may be asked the following:

♦ Whether all tutors are teachers. You need to explain that you only accept applications from teachers and experienced tutors.

♦ How the tutors are vetted by the agency. Reassure clients that a fully comprehensive application form is completed by each tutor and two references are provided. Point out that the relationship between client and tutor is based on mutual trust. However, while clients have the benefit of the agency's vetting procedure, tutors take clients on trust alone.

♦ How long tutors have taught at their current school, their age, their teaching track record. Advise clients to ask tutors these questions themselves.

A WORD OF CAUTION

You may receive requests for tutors from students themselves, either because they speak better English than their parents or because their parents have given them permission to book their own tutor. However, do ensure at this initial stage that you actually speak to the person who will be paying for the tuition, otherwise you may find that the parents had not in fact agreed to pay or that they had already found a tutor elsewhere.

At this point you are ready to match pupils to tutors.

6

CLINCHING THE DEAL

'Never leave till tomorrow that which you can do today.'

BENJAMIN FRANKLIN

Your agency will be much more successful than other agencies if you don't leave things to chance, you take total control and see the deal through.

LINKING CLIENTS TO TUTORS

Clients sometimes approach more than one agency at the same time. Speed and efficiency are the essence of a successful tutoring agency and ensure that your agency gets the business.

Speed

When speaking to clients, give them a clear timescale of how long it will take to find them a tutor. This should be no longer than two days. You then need to contact a suitable tutor immediately and ask them to ring the client as soon as possible. If this process is taking longer than you expected, perhaps because the tutor cannot ring straight away, keep the client informed of the situation. Otherwise, they may think that you have been unable to find them a tutor and consequently you may lose the booking. However, do not give them the tutor's telephone number, because it is important that you keep control of the situation at every stage of the process.

Efficiency

Your agency should pride itself on matching pupils to tutors and in paying attention to detail. This largely depends upon making a note on the booking form of everything a client tells you about their child and passing this information on to the tutor. It is also dependent upon you knowing as much as possible about the tutor. Paying attention to minor details, such as when the tutor is on holiday, can prove to be as important as major details such as which period in history they teach.

Seeing the deal through and keeping control

Keep control of the situation by monitoring it carefully. It is not enough to put tutors in touch with clients and to assume that the deal is done. You need to pursue tutors if they do not ring back to let you know what is happening. Expect tutors to call back the same day or the next day at the latest. If necessary, you can get this information from clients. If they have not yet heard from the tutor, they will be reassured that you are dealing with their booking.

If a tutor tells you that things did not work out, call the client to find out why. It may be that the client did not like the sound of that tutor and felt embarrassed about asking for another. Tell the tutor that you will be asking the client why they have changed their mind. Letting tutors know that you keep your eye on each potential booking stops them setting up private deals.

If arrangements become confused, take control. Tutors and clients leaving each other messages on answerphones can prolong the process unnecessarily. This is when you need to step in and tell a tutor to leave a specific telephone message letting the client know when they will be available to receive their phone call.

Confirmation in writing to clients

Confirmation in writing to clients is an important and effective part of the process, and one that will set your agency apart from other agencies. Once tutors have informed you that lessons are to go ahead, send clients a client information form.

EDGSTONE TUTORS
69 High Road, Edgstone, London E12 9SZ
Telephone 020 8666 4222

CLIENT INFORMATION FORM

Thank you for applying to our agency for a tutor. If you have any
problems or queries please do not hesitate to contact the agency.

SUBJECT

TUTOR

PLEASE READ THE FOLLOWING CAREFULLY

PAYMENT OF FEES
♦ The administration fee of £5 is now due and should be paid to the tutor at the
end of the first lesson.
♦ Tutors are paid by the client at the end of each lesson.
♦ The lesson fees are £20 per hour for primary level tuition, £22 from year 7 to
GCSE level, £24 for AS- and A- level, £24 for Special Needs and £25 for Uni-
versity level.
♦ Students sharing lessons. The first student pays full amount, those sharing
pay half. The total fee is then divided equally amongst the students so that each
one benefits from a discount.
♦ The client will be asked to sign the tutor's timesheet at the end of each lesson.
♦ Tutors may ask for an additional £2.00 for travelling to the pupil's home.

CANCELLATION
♦ Make a note of your tutor's telephone number in case you have to contact him/
her.
♦ 24 hours' notice of cancellation is required by both tutor and client.
♦ If 24 hours' notice is not given to the tutors they may, at their discretion, charge
a cancellation fee.

PLEASE NOTE
We are an introduction agency only. Whilst we make every effort to secure
the best services for our clients, Edgstone Tutors cannot, under any
circumstances, accept responsibility for the acts or omissions of the tutor
introduced or for any loss, expense or damage incurred.

Fig. 22. Client information form.

Whereas many agencies rely on telephone confirmation only, clients do appreciate having this information in writing. Clients may not have kept the newspaper where they first saw your advertisement therefore this form is important because it provides them with a written record of your name and telephone number. This well thought-out form also confirms the subject to be taught and the level, the name of their tutor, the cost of lessons and the process of payment. It encourages clients to make a note of the tutor's telephone number at this stage, but it does not give personal details about the tutor or their work history. Should clients want this information, they can ask the tutor directly. In addition, this form sets out clear and simple guidelines on cancellation of lessons and the agency's responsibility to clients.

Confirmation in writing to tutors

Confirmation in writing to tutors is done by sending them a small supply of timesheets (Figure 23).

These timesheets have been designed to inform the agency of how many lessons tutors have given, how much commission is due to the agency and whether or not the tuition is to continue. Do not send too many in one go; in this way tutors will need to contact you from time to time to ask for more and this is a useful way of keeping in touch.

All new clients pay an administration fee of £5 to the agency. With the timesheets, you need to enclose an administration fee slip (Figure 24) to remind tutors to collect this fee at the end of the first lesson on behalf of the agency.

KEEPING A RECORD OF THE DEAL

This is an essential part of keeping control of your business.

You need to keep a record of every new client on the tutor database or in the tutors' card index filing system. This will ensure that at the end of each month when tutors send in their commission (see Chapter 8), you can check that they have paid for each client you have allocated to them.

EDGSTONE TUTORS
69 High Road, Edgstone, London E12 9SZ
020 8666 4222

TIMESHEET

NAME OF TUTOR ....
(first name and surname)

NAME OF STUDENT ....
(first name and surname)

Commision for the month of ....

Date of lesson	Lesson duration	Fee paid	Signature of client
1			
2			
3			
4			

Total commission to agency: £ ....

Is this tuition continuing?   YES/NO   Signature of tutor: ....

PLEASE RETURN YOUR COMPLETED TIMESHEETS PROMPTLY AT THE END OF EACH MONTH.

Fig. 23. Timesheet.

Edgstone Tutors
69 High Road, Edgstone, London E12 9SZ
020 8666 4444

ADMINISTRATION FEE SLIP

The administration fee of £5 payable by the client should be collected by you at the end of the first lesson and sent to the agency with your commission at the end of the month.

Please let the agency know when this course of tuition comes to an end.

Fig. 24. Administration fee slip.

You also need to have a client list either on computer or in a client card index filing system so that you have a record of current and recent clients. You may, for example, need to refer to this if a client contacts the agency again after a period of time asking for the same tutor as before.

As soon as the deal is set up you need to add tutors' names to a computer spreadsheet or to a monthly accounts list so that you know which tutors should be sending you commission (see Chapter 9).

CLIENT LIST

ABLE Mr 60 Field Lane, Edgstone E12 2PY 8666 1817 (H) 8666 8001 (W)
07905 720885 (M) £5 PAID
A-level Biology and A Chemistry revision course at Easter
TUTOR: FOR BIOLOGY DR KOTAL 1st LESSON MID-MARCH 2005 BOOKING
12.03.05
EASTER REVISION – MARTIN SPYERS.

ADDLEY Samantha 137 Teddingon Road, Stanbridge E10 8TZ 8667 4490 (H)
07914 2192301 (M)
2 sons at Grace Hall School aged 8 and 10 for Maths, English, Science and
History
TUTOR: FATIMA SHAH 1st LESSON 23.04.04 BOOKING 21.04.04 AND
RESTARTED 16.08.05

AHSAK Mr 2 Cider Avenue, Edgstone E12 9AR 8666 393911
Daughter Yr 5 for Maths and English
TUTOR: MRS FULLER 1st LESSON 08.10.05 BOOKING 05.10.05

AITCHISON Claire 54 Glasgow Road, Carlton E20 3NU 8669 1490 £5 PAID
Son Yr 11 poor GCSE mock results at Carlton Grammar
Maths, English and Business Studies
TUTOR: MATHS: GARRY FITKIN 1st LESSON 15.02.05 BOOKING 07.02.05
TUTOR: BUSINESS STUDIES: CHRIS BRYAN 1st LESSON FEB 05

ALDERMAN Mrs 10 Holton Road, Carlton E20 5JB 8669 0821
Daughter Freya aged 11 Yr 6 for Maths and English
TUTOR: STEVE GILL 1st LESSON 17.06.06 BOOKING 11.06.06

ALI Mr 21 Upminster Close, Edgstone E12 5PU 8666 2234
A-level Maths stats for daughter
TUTOR: Mr HICKMAN 1st LESSON 13.09.04 BOOKING 09.09.04
AND MARCH 2005 MR T. SHAH FOR A-LEVEL BIOLOGY BOOKING 26.02.05

Fig. 25. Client list.

AMIN Mr 17 Woodland Close, Edgstone E12 0JP 8666 1879
Spanish Yr 10 for daughter
TUTOR: JEMMA KAVAS 1st LESSON 12.10.02 BOOKING 10.10.02
AND MARCH 2004 SUNITA PATEL FOR GCSE MATHS YR 11 BOOKING
07.03.04
CHANGED TO CLIVE COLLINS 02.04.04

ANSELL Sally 72 Praed Street, Stanbridge E10 3NU 8667 1215 (H) 8667 2138
(W) 07719 486170 (M)
Son Yr 11 poor GCSE mock exam results at Stanbridge Grammar
Business Studies
Maths – TUTOR: SUNITA PATEL 1st LESSON 15.02.05
English
BOOKING 7.02.05

ARNOLD Sarah 84 High Road, Stanbridge E10 5AF 8667 2737
A-level English AQA Board this weekend only
TUTOR: NICK LEVY 1st LESSON 30.01.05 BOOKING 29.01.05

ASHCROFT Mr 191 Cloister Road, Edgstone E12 0TU 8666 3812
A-level Physics son
TUTOR: MISS DURBAN 1st LESSON AFTER EASTER 2005 BOOKING 22.02.05

AVER Alison 57 Rutland Street, Carlton E20 7PG. 8669 4634
Thomas aged 13 – Maths and Steven – English and Maths for 14+ SATS
TUTOR: JAMES MERTON 1st LESSON 16.11.05 BOOKING 10.11.05

Fig. 25. (continued).

7

WHEN THE TUITION ENDS

'Even the woodpecker owes his success to the fact that he uses his head and keeps pecking away until he finishes the job he starts.'

COLEMAN COX

FINDING OUT WHEN TUITION ENDS

You need to know when tuition has finished so that you are aware that a tutor will no longer be sending you commission for a particular client.

How you receive this information

There are several ways in which you will find this out:

- The completed timesheets will inform you. On every timesheet tutors answer the question 'Is this tuition continuing? YES/NO'.

- The tutor may telephone to let you know.

- The client may telephone to say that they are finishing with the tutor.

If you have not been informed that the tuition has come to an end but you do not receive commission for a particular client, ring the tutor to find out why. It may be that the tutor has forgotten to send the commission for that client or that they omitted to inform you that the tuition has ended. This will emphasise the fact to tutors that you keep a close eye on every aspect of the business.

You also need to know when the tuition has finished so that you can send the client an end of tuition slip (see Figure 26) which will encourage them to use your agency again. Take the opportunity to advertise your agency by enclosing some leaflets.

Edgstone Tutors

69 High Road, Edgstone, London E12 9SZ

020 8666 4222

END OF TUITION SLIP

The tuition you have requested has now been completed. We hope that you have benefited from it.

Please recommend us to friends and colleagues. If you need our assistance again, do not hesitate to contact us.

Fig. 26. End of tuition slip.

If you are concerned about a client who has stopped tuition unexpectedly, it is worth ringing the client to find out why. It may be that they did not like their tutor and felt awkward about asking for a replacement. This is a good public-relations exercise and will stop the client from going to a different agency.

When you are certain that the tuition has ended

♦ Put the word FINISHED under the client's name on the client list.

♦ Move the client's name in the tutor's entry on the database from the Current Client field to the Past Client field.

♦ Remember, if you are using a card index system, write FINISHED on both the tutor's card and the client's card.

8

MAKING YOUR MONEY

'Wealth, like happiness, is never attained when sought after directly. It comes as a by-product of providing a useful service.'

HENRY FORD

METHODS BY WHICH TUTORING AGENCIES MAKE THEIR MONEY

Some agencies are paid directly by clients. This system is costly, time-consuming and complicated. The agency would first have to establish how many lessons every tutor had given every client, then bill every client individually each month. If clients did not pay, even though they had had the lessons, the agency would then have to initiate measures to recover the fees. In addition, if clients pay the agency, the agency then needs to pay the tutors, thus making tutors employees of the agency.

Other agencies are paid a lump sum by every tutor who joins their agency in anticipation of work, but tutors are reluctant to pay money up front.

Payment to your tutoring agency

The simplest, most reliable and efficient way of making your money is for the agency to be paid commission by tutors for each lesson taught.

Tutors are paid their lesson fees, including the agency commission, by clients at the end of each lesson. This system works extremely well because, as with any service industry, clients expect to pay immediately for the service they have received. At the end of each month, tutors send the agency the accumulated commission and any administration fees collected, together with completed timesheets. Tutors can be relied upon to send in the commission because they depend upon the agency for more work. This method of payment guarantees the tutors' self-employed status and relieves the agency from the burden of being an employer.

You will know which tutors should be paying commission to the agency by referring to the spreadsheet or the monthly accounts list (see Chapter 9, Figure 29).

Tutors are given two weeks from the end of the month to pay the agency commission, after which time they are reminded by telephone. If after another week commission is not forthcoming, tutors are sent a written reminder (see Figure 27).

Edgstone Tutors

69 High Road, Edgstone, London E12 9SZ

020 8666 4222

FIRST REMINDER

Could you please let us have timesheets and commission for the months of
_____ so that we can finalise our end-of-month accounts.
With thanks.

Fig. 27. Commission: first reminder.

If commission is still outstanding two weeks after this reminder then a final notification is sent (see Figure 28).

Tutors who have worked for the agency for some time can be allowed a little more leeway. However, do not allow this to go on for more than two months. Do not allow new tutors to fall behind at all in their payment of commission. As a last resort you may need to call upon the services of a debt collection agency (see Chapter 12, p. 73).

Edgstone Tutors
69 High Road, Edgstone, London E12 9SZ
020 8666 4222

FINAL NOTIFICATION

The outstanding commission owed to Edgstone Tutors should be sent **by return of post. No further reminder will be sent.** Non-payment will result in the following procedure:

- Letter to referees informing of non-payment.
- Letter to debt collection agency to instigate proceedings.

Fig. 28. Commission: final notification.

SETTING THE RATES

When setting the charges for lessons, a balance needs to be achieved between a fair rate of pay for tutors and an affordable fee for clients. This needs to be competitive with other local agencies. You need to make it clear to clients and tutors that all rates are fixed by the agency and they cannot negotiate their own deal. Special terms must be approved by the agency.

These rates should be reviewed annually in line with other local agencies. As a guideline the 2006 rates were:

Cost of hourly lessons including agency commission

Primary level (Yrs 1–6)	£20
Secondary/GCSE level (Yrs 7–11)	£22
AS-/A-level (Yrs 12–13)	£24
Special needs	£24
University level	£25

Agency commission

Many agencies charge their tutors commission on a sliding scale. For example A-level £4.00, GCSE £3.25, Primary £2.75. Some also have a policy of reducing commission after a certain number of lessons, for example commission on the first 20 lessons is £4 and subsequent lessons £3.50. These systems are unnecessarily complicated for both agency and tutors.

A blanket charge of £3 per lesson, whatever the level, however many lessons are given, is by far the easiest system.

EXCEPTIONS TO THE RULE

Shared lessons

Parents may ask for their child to be tutored together with a friend or friends who are at the same academic level. A simple formula for setting the rates for shared lessons has been devised. The first student pays the full rate and additional students each pay half. The total fee is then divided equally amongst the students so that each one benefits from a discount. The agency commission is paid pro rata.

Twins

Twins may be tutored together but this is only advisable if they are at the same academic level. In this case, the rate is the full fee for the first twin plus £5 for the second twin. The agency commission remains at £3 in total.

Block bookings

When a request is made for a large number of lessons over a short period of time, for example ten lessons over the two-week Christmas holiday period, a discount of approximately 10% may be offered to clients. Both the tutor and the agency take a 10% reduction. For example, for ten hours of A-level lessons the cost to the client is reduced from £240 to £216. The agency commission is reduced from £30 to £27. However, with block bookings, it is vital that the total fee is paid in advance.

The fees for the following courses are set out in Chapter 10, pp. 61 and 63: revision courses, language courses, pre-school reading courses.

ADMINISTRATION FEE

This is a one-off payment by clients irrespective of how many times they use the agency. This fee covers the cost of telephone calls and postage. It is collected by tutors at the end of the first lesson. Tutors have been informed of this administration fee on their information for tutors form (see Chapter 3, Figure 7). Clients are informed of this fee when they book lessons and it is confirmed in writing on the client information form (see Chapter 6, Figure 22). If clients are hesitant about booking lessons and you suspect it is because of this small additional cost, you could at your discretion waive the administration fee. It is worth sacrificing £5 for the sake of goodwill. If you do not charge the administration fee, remember to cross out the sentence about the fee on the client information form.

9

FINANCIAL MATTERS

'Happiness is not in the mere possession of money; it lies in the joy of achievement, in the thrill of creative effort.'

FRANKLIN D. ROOSEVELT

KEEPING ACCOUNTS

This need not be a complicated procedure but it does need to be accurate, organised and up to date, because it is *key* to keeping control of your income.

Income

You need to know, every month, which tutors should be sending you commission, so that if you do not receive money from a tutor, from whom you had expected payment, you will know that you need to remind them to pay.

Expenditure

Keep careful account of all money spent on behalf of your agency. Make sure you keep receipts, as all business expenses are tax deductible.

Advertising is the main expense of this business. Other outgoings, which include photocopying, stationery, stamps and telephone bills are minimal. Take advantage of contacts who have access to reduced price photocopying and stationery.

Manual accounting

When working with a manual system, you need to have a monthly accounts list on which you keep the name of every tutor who has taught for you in that month. At the end of each month, when tutors send in their timesheets and cheques, put the amount of money paid by each tutor next to their name, so that you can see at a glance which tutors have taught lessons and have sent in the agency commission and which tutors have taught lessons but have not paid the agency commission.

Every month you need to update this list by adding the names of any tutors who started teaching in the current month and by removing the names of those tutors who finished teaching in the previous month.

At the end of each month, pay all cheques into the bank and enter the total amount received for the month into the credit column of an accounts book. At the same time add up the total amount of expenditure for the month and enter it into the debit column of an accounts book. This simple method of accounting enables you to keep an accurate record of all income and expenditure.

Computerised accounting

When tutors start tutoring for your agency, you need to put their names onto a spreadsheet (see Figure 29). Put the letters SS (Student Started) in the column for the relevant month.

At the end of each month, when tutors send in their timesheets and cheques, put the amount of money paid by each tutor next to their name on the spreadsheet in the relevant column for that month, so that you can easily see which tutors have taught lessons and sent in their commission, and which tutors have taught lessons but have not paid the agency commission. This enables you to keep an accurate record of all tutors who have taught for you at any time during each financial year and the amount they have paid.

When tutors finish tutoring all their students you need to make a note of this on the spreadsheet by putting the letters FIN (FINISHED) in the column for the relevant month, so that you know not to expect any more payments from particular tutors (see Figure 29).

SPREADSHEET ACCOUNTS 2000

	01/04/2000	01/05/2000	01/06/2000
ALBERTS	12	18	9FIN
ARMSTRONG	30	30	27
ARNOLD	40	21	21
ATKINSON	12	12	18
ATRIBE	24	24	30
BARBER	12	12	12
BARNSTONE	15	18	18
BASIELLI	18	51	55
BOURTON	SS	12	12
BRITTAN	0	SS	12
BUNTER R	18	12	18
CASALLIS	9	9	9
CHELMES	18	18	18
CLASPER	27	45	15FIN
COURZON	SS	15	18
CRABB	18	27	27FIN
CRENDAL	16	15	15
CROSS	39	0	9FIN
CURTLEY	12	12	12
DAVIS	18	15	15
DEKKA	47	32	15FIN
DILBY	21	21	18
ELTON	21	0	30
ENGELS	18	18	18
ESTELLE	0	0	99
FALLAN	0	36	40
FARMER	12	6	6FIN
FERN	4	8	4
FERGUSON	4	12	12
FOSTER	12	0	49

Fig. 29. Accounts spreadsheet

At the end of each month pay all cheques into the bank and enter the total amount received for the month into the credit column of a computer accounts file. At the same time add up the total amount of expenditure for the month and enter it into the debit column of a computer accounts file (see Figure 30).

TAX RETURNS

Although self-assessment for income tax is not too complicated, you may prefer to use the services of an accountant to prepare your end-of - year accounts for the Inland Revenue, particularly when first starting your business. They could also give you good advice about personal tax payments and pension plans.

BANKING

It is worthwhile researching what high street banks and building societies offer small businesses in the way of free banking. If you take advantage of the offer of two years' free banking at one bank, you might want to consider changing banks after this period in order to take advantage of a further period of free banking.

TELEPHONE SYSTEMS

To get the very best deal for your business, speak to your telephone service provider to see if there is a deal to be negotiated. Your agency is heavily dependent upon having an economical telephone system, and you may find that the cheapest way of operating your telephone is to pay a small quarterly fee in exchange for free local and national calls.

When setting up your business you do not need to have a separate telephone number; you can simply use your existing home number. Once your business becomes busy you may wish to have a dedicated business line.

TOTAL ACCOUNTS 6 APRIL 2000–5 APRIL 2001

Date		Debit	Credit	TOTAL
APRIL 2000 TOTAL CARRIED OVER FROM END OF LAST FINANCIAL YEAR, i.e. 1999–2000				**793.00**
April				
7	Paid in	–	560.00	1353.00
10	Withdrawal	270.00	–	1083.00
22	Payment for advertising	115.00	–	968.00
22	Paid in	–	366.00	1334.00
23	Withdrawal	360.00	–	974.00
May				
2	Withdrawal	360.00	–	614.00
5	Paid in	–	527.00	1141.00
15	Paid in	–	554.00	1695.00
25	Payment for advertising	115.00	–	1580.00

Fig. 30. Total accounts

In order not to miss any calls when you are not at home there are two options. The first option is to set up an answering service with your telephone service provider or you can have an answering machine. Consider carefully the message that you leave. Simply saying '8666 4222, please leave a message after the tone', will deter prospective clients from waiting for a return call from you and they may ring another agency. A friendly, informative message encourages callers to wait for your return call. For example, 'This is Edgstone Tutors. I'm sorry there's no one here to take your call at the moment, but do please leave your name, telephone number and a brief message, if you wish, and I will return your call today.' The second option is to put your telephone on call divert either to your mobile telephone or to a landline wherever you are.

If you decide to have a dedicated business line you may think that Freephone will encourage clients to ring your agency. However, this is an unnecessary expense as clients will not be deterred from choosing your agency by the cost of a telephone call.

10

EXPANDING YOUR BUSINESS

'Ambition is the path to success.
Persistence is the vehicle you arrive in.'

BILL BRADLEY

DIVERSIFICATION

Once your tutoring agency is established and running smoothly, you can think about expanding the business and increasing your income. The core business can be used as a springboard to other opportunities, and the confidence you have gained will allow you to try out your own ideas. Be prepared as well to listen to tutors' ideas and suggestions for special teaching packages or courses. The possibilities are endless. You might like to consider some of these options:

Revision courses

GCSE and A-level revision courses taking place during Christmas, half-term and Easter school holidays are in great demand and often oversubscribed. Choose your subjects carefully. Popular subjects are double Science, Maths and English at GCSE level and A-level Maths and Sciences. You may have tutors offering to run courses in other subjects such as Geography, History and English A-level but it would be difficult to run courses in these subjects as syllabuses vary enormously.

The first thing to do is to contact your registered tutors who teach these subjects and who you think might like to run a holiday revision course in their own home. It may be that some of your tutors have already approached you about teaching a revision course. Next, establish with each tutor the dates and times of their course and the maximum and minimum number of pupils they will take. Try to co-ordinate courses so that pupils can, if they wish, attend more than one. You need to change your weekly advertisement to include the words holiday revision courses (see Chapter 4, Figure 20). However, do not do this too far in advance of the date of the course; two or three weeks before will suffice as people book notoriously late. In addition, tutors teaching these courses should be encouraged to help with the advertising process by sending leaflets to their local schools, putting posters in their libraries and spreading the word amongst their current pupils.

Now that you have in place tutors, timetables and advertising, you need to set the rates. A simple formula for a GCSE course is £120 for ten hours of tuition. A non-refundable deposit of £20 is paid to the agency and is the total agency fee, the remaining £100 is paid to the tutor at the first lesson. The cost of an A-level course is £160 and the system of payment is the same, with a £20 deposit to the agency and the remainder payable to the tutor.

At this point prepare a booking form to be sent in response to clients' enquiries (see Figure 31). If tutors' current pupils wish to take part in their revision course, they must nevertheless go through the same booking process. The booking form is designed so that only one form is needed for GCSE level and one form for A-level no matter how many courses you are providing. The name and address of the tutor does not appear on the form. These measures ensure that the agency stays in control of the whole procedure.

Once the booking forms are returned with the non-refundable deposits, ring the tutors to ask them to contact the clients. This is so that they can introduce themselves and give the address at which the course is taking place. At the same time, they can take the opportunity to speak to the pupil to find out what they are hoping to get from the course and to tell them what they need to bring with them to each lesson.

Last-minute tuition
Some agencies are unwilling to allocate tutors to pupils very late in the

EDGSTONE TUTORS
69 High Road, Edgstone, London E12 9SZ
020 8666 4222

REVISION COURSE TIMETABLE AND BOOKING FORM

MATHS COURSE		ENGLISH COURSE	
22–24 March		29–31 March	
Mon 21	–	Mon 28	BANK HOLIDAY
Tues 22	9–12.30	Tues 29	9–12.30
Wed 23	9–12.30	Wed 30	9–12.30
Thurs 24	9–12.00	Thurs 31	9–12.00
Fri 25	BANK HOLIDAY	Fri 1	–

COST PER 10-HOUR COURSE = £120 in total.
A £20 non-refundable deposit payable to Edgstone Tutors is required when booking.
The balance is paid to the tutor at the first lesson.

To book your place on a course(s) please complete and return the tear off booking
form and return it to Edgstone Tutors with a cheque for your deposit.

✄ -

Revision Courses – Booking Form

Please tick the course/courses you wish to book:

MATHS ☐   ENGLISH ☐

Name of student: ....

Address: ....

....

Telephone number: ....

Signed: ....   Dated: ....

Enc. Cheque for £20 per course payable to Edgstone Tutors.

Fig. 31. Revision course timetable and booking form.

day, for example on a Friday when the student has an exam on the following Monday. If you spend a little time finding a tutor, even if they can only fit in a few hours' tuition over the weekend, not only is it helpful to the student but it is also an excellent PR exercise for your agency and may lead to further bookings. The student may decide to book a course of lessons in a different subject or he may have six brothers and sisters who use the agency at a future date!

Language courses

'Get by in Italian/Spanish/French' daytime or evening group language courses for adults travelling abroad are increasingly popular. As with revision courses, the agency keeps control of the whole process by selecting tutors, arranging timetables, advertising, setting the rates and taking the bookings. The perfect time to start these courses is immediately after Easter. Add an extra line to your weekly advertisement 'Get by in Italian/Spanish/French' several weeks before Easter. A competitive rate for a 20-hour course spread over ten weeks is £200. A non-refundable deposit of £40 is the agency fee.

Pre-school reading courses

Parents are keen to give their children a good start in reading and you can meet the demand for pre-school learning by arranging morning or afternoon group lessons for three to five year olds. As these courses could run throughout the year, a perfect place for advertising is nursery-school noticeboards. The cost for a weekly 45 minute lesson is £100 per term. A non-refundable deposit of £20 is the agency fee.

Tuition for children out of school

There are an increasingly large number of children who, for one reason or another, are not attending school. They may be recovering from an illness, their parents may have withdrawn them from one school but not yet found a new one, or they may have been bullied and are refusing to attend school. Three one-hour lessons per week for a primary school child, taught by one teacher, would help them to keep up with all subjects. This is not the same for a child at secondary school, whose parents may ask you to provide tutors in the nine different subjects that the child has been studying. It is unlikely that they will have considered the cost of this and you should advise them to concentrate on the core subjects of Maths, Science and English. Lessons are charged at your normal hourly rates.

Supply teaching

Agencies which provide supply teachers to local authority schools tend to be separate entities from tutoring agencies, which supply local tutors to clients on a one-to-one basis. This is because supply teachers are generally employed by the agency and this completely changes the dynamics of the business. Once an agency becomes an employer they become responsible for the tax and national insurance of their employees. However, this is an extremely lucrative business and you may wish to consider branching out in this way.

Holiday courses

There is a growing trend for parents to send their children on activity holiday courses: football training, horse riding, gymnastics, art workshops or sailing. This is a good way to make money but requires months of planning and substantial financial outlay both to hire premises and to purchase an excellent insurance policy. These holiday courses are another way in which you may wish to branch out from your core business.

11
RESOURCES FOR TUTORS

'Books are the compasses and telescopes and sextants and charts which other men have prepared to help us navigate the seas of life.'

ANON

TEACHING MATERIALS

Encourage your tutors to supply their own resources. They may assume that pupils will have their own textbooks to use during lessons but parents will expect tutors to give a well-prepared lesson and to have a variety of books and exam papers.

Teachers who are currently working in schools will have no problem gaining access to appropriate material. Tutors may ask for your advice about where they can find the necessary resources for their level of tuition and you can point them in the right direction. Larger local libraries have a good selection of teaching resources and also provide internet access. The internet is an excellent source of information about examinations at all levels.

Exam papers

GCSE and A-level exam papers can be purchased for a small cost from examination boards along with a current syllabus and notes for teachers. Tutors teaching GCSE and A-level must have these resources, which they can then use many times over.

Examination boards

Assessment and Qualifications Alliance (AQA North)
Devas Street
Manchester M15 6EX
Tel: 0161 953 1180
Fax: 0161 455 5444
Website: www.aqa.org.uk

Assessment and Qualifications Alliance (AQA South)
Stag Hill House
Guildford
Surrey GU2 5XJ
Tel: 01483 506 506
Fax: 01483 300 152
Website www.aqa.org.uk

City & Guilds
1 Giltspur Street
London EC1A 9DD
Tel: 020 7294 2800
Fax: 020 7294 2400
Website: www.city-and-guilds.co.uk

Edexcel
190 High Holborn
London WC1V 7BH
Tel: 0870 240 9800
Fax: 020 7190 5700
Minicom: 0870 240 3941
Website: www.edexcel.org.uk

Northern Ireland Council for the Curriculum Examinations and Assessment (CCEA)
29 Clarendon Road
Belfast BT1 3BG
Tel: 02890 261 200

Fax: 02890 261 234
Website: www.ccea.org.uk

Oxford, Cambridge and RSA (OCR)
Syndicate Buildings
1 Hills Road
Cambridge CB1 2EU
Tel: 01223 553 998
Fax: 01223 552 627
Website: www.ocr.org.uk

Scottish Qualifications Authority (SQA)
Hanover House
24 Douglas Street
Glasgow G2 7NQ
Tel: 0845 279 1000
Fax: 0141 242 2244
Website: www.sqa.org.uk

Welsh Joint Education Committee
245 Western Avenue
Cardiff
CF5 2YX
Tel: 02920 265 000 (Main switchboard) or Tel: 02920 265 155 (GCSE administration)
Website: www.wjec.co.uk

Joint Council for Qualifications (JCQ)
Veritas House
125 Finsbury Pavement
London EC2A 1NQ
Tel: 020 7638 4135
Website: www.jcq.org.uk

International Baccalaureate Organisation
Peterson House
Malthouse Avenue

Cardiff Gate
Cardiff
Wales CF23 8GL
Tel: 0292 0547 777
Fax: 0292 0547 778
Website: www.ibo.org

SATs papers are available from WH Smith and other large bookshops.

Entrance exam papers for independent or selective schools can be difficult to obtain. Some schools have a policy of not publishing their exam papers. However, if you can get a supply of entrance exam papers from schools which either give them or sell them to parents, you can photocopy these and lend them to your tutors. This will give good primary school teachers confidence to take on exam coaching if they wish, even though they have not done so before.

Keep up to date and inform your tutors of changes to exam procedures as schools will vary their requirements from year to year. For example, one year a school may set exams in English and Maths. The following year, they may ask pupils to do a verbal or non-verbal reasoning paper and then call the pupils back to sit exams in English and Maths if they have scored highly in the preliminary papers. It is worth a telephone call to the different schools to check on these requirements and to ask for past papers.

Some schools, predominantly boarding or ex-boarding schools, still use the common entrance examination system at 11+ or 13+. Whereas entrance exam papers for independent or selective schools may differ for every school, common entrance examination papers will be the same for all schools. These papers can be purchased from:

Independent Schools Examinations Board (ISEB)
Jordan House
Christchurch Road
New Milton BH25 6QJ
Tel: 01425 621111

Fax: 01425 620044
Website: www.iseb.co.uk/

Books

New tutors joining your agency might like some guidelines regarding which books to use and what level of achievement is required for different age groups. If you cannot provide this information yourself, put them in touch with one of your experienced tutors who is currently teaching in a school. Revision books such as Letts or Collins Guides might initially help a new GCSE or A-level tutor to gauge the required level.

Reading lists

Primary-level tutors must be familiar with good quality children's reading books so that they can recommend them to their pupils. It would be helpful if you had obtained reading lists for children of all ages from local schools. Most schools offer these annually to the parents of their pupils.

12

TROUBLESHOOTING

'*Dealing with people is probably the biggest problem you face, especially if you are in business.*'

DALE CARNAGIE

PROBLEMS YOU MAY ENCOUNTER

This is a business which presents very few problems. However, we have tried in this chapter to pre-empt as many as possible of the difficulties that you may come across.

Demanding or difficult clients

Try to satisfy the needs of clients as far as possible. Clients may specifically request a female tutor, or a young tutor, or someone who is currently teaching in a school. These are reasonable requests with which you could easily comply. However, if clients become too demanding, and it is impossible to meet their requests, be prepared to turn them down. For example, a client may tell you that the only time their child is free to have a lesson is on Sunday afternoons from 4.50 p.m. to 5.50 p.m. If you cannot persuade the client to be a little more flexible, you may find that it is not worth your while searching for the one tutor from the many you have available who is prepared to work at that time.

If you have wasted a lot of time with a very difficult client who, despite your efforts, did not book a tutor, make a note of the client's name so that, should they come back to the agency at a future date, you will know not to spend too much time trying to accommodate them.

Difficulties between student and tutor

Clients may be under the impression that you will offer them a selection of tutors to choose from. You need to explain that you will match a child's needs very carefully to a tutor. However, in the unlikely event that a pupil does not get on well with a tutor after several lessons, be prepared to find an alternative tutor. If this happens again with the same pupil, it may become obvious to you that you did find the right tutors but in fact the child simply does not want lessons. In this situation, it is not sensible to keep on supplying tutors and you need to discuss this with the parents who may not have realised that there is a problem.

If clients request a change of tutor after only one lesson, you might suggest that they have another one or two lessons, giving the pupil and tutor a better chance to get to know each other. It is surprising how often this resolves the problem, because a tutor might use the first lesson to assess their pupil's ability, whereas the pupil might have unrealistic expectations of that lesson, thinking that it could resolve all their difficulties with A-level statistics!

If a particular tutor fails to keep pupils for more than one or two lessons, it is worth contacting the pupils to see what the problem was. If it transpires that he is not a good teacher, it is not worth using this tutor again.

Cancellation of lessons

Written information is given to both tutors and clients regarding the cancellation of lessons, and both the client information form and the information for tutors form state that '24 hours' notice of cancellation is required of both tutor and client'. Both forms state that if notice is not given 'tutors may at their discretion charge a cancellation fee'. However, you may occasionally be called upon to mediate between tutor and client. For example, a tutor may turn up for a lesson only to find that there is no one at home. Subsequently, he asks the parents for a cancellation fee to which he is entitled. The parents refuse to pay the fee because they were called away at short notice to attend to a sick relative and did not have either the agency or tutor's telephone number with them so that they could cancel the lesson. As a general rule, you should support your tutors who lose time and money if pupils do not give sufficient notice of lesson cancellation. However, when there is a genuine excuse, try to persuade the tutor to give the client another chance but to make it clear that this must not happen again.

If a tutor is unreliable, repeatedly turning up late for lessons or not turning up at all or changing the day and time of lessons, then it is not worth using them, however good a teacher they are, because they will lose you clients.

Clients who do not pay

The agency makes it abundantly clear to tutors that they are responsible for the collection of fees at the end of every lesson. If they ring you and say that a client has not paid them, suggest that they make it clear to the client either in writing or by telephone that they must be given the fee owed before the beginning of the next lesson. They should not teach another lesson until the fee is paid. However, if a tutor does not let you know until they are owed for several lessons, then you might agree to try and get the money on their behalf. Ringing the client and appealing to their better nature is often successful, even when a tutor has failed to get the money owed. If all attempts fail, however upset your tutor feels, there is a point at which you need to persuade them to accept the situation, because any further attempts to recover fees will be time-consuming and costly.

Clients who try to strike bargains

It is not uncommon for a client to ring, book a tutor and then ask you if you can make the lessons a little cheaper. You need to make it absolutely clear that the prices are non-negotiable and have been set so that tutors earn a fair fee and clients are not overcharged. Explain to clients that the cost of lessons is very small compared to other professional fees. Clients may try to strike a deal with tutors. As a general rule tutors must stick to the prescribed rates unless, in special circumstances, a different rate has been negotiated through the agency.

Tutors who do not pay

The process by which this problem is dealt with is outlined in Chapter 8. If, however, the tutor fails to pay commission owed to the agency after you have sent a final notification of payment, you need to make a claim through the small claims court. As this involves a lot of time, you may decide instead to use the services of a debt collection agency who will deal with this matter on your behalf. However, trying to recover this debt is an extremely lengthy and costly process which involves debt collection agency fees and court costs. Even when the court rules in your favour, there is no guarantee that the tutor will pay. In order to collect payment, bailiffs are employed at extra cost to you and they will only enter commercial premises, not private property, to obtain goods to the value of the debt. It is most unlikely that your tutor has commercial premises and so the debt will remain unpaid. It is therefore imperative that you do not allow tutors to owe you money.

13

TUTORS

'Good teaching is one-fourth preparation and three-fourths theatre.'

GAIL GODWIN

In an ideal world the tutoring agent would meet all tutors before registering them, but in reality this is not possible. Since all contact is by telephone, it is imperative to speak to the person wanting to be a tutor and not someone asking for an application form on their behalf. Whilst the agent will be able to make an initial assessment about tutors who may have excellent qualifications and look good on paper, the proof of the pudding is in the eating. It is feedback from clients that will tell the agent whether or not a particular tutor is a good teacher. However, bear in mind that clients' opinions will be subjective.

ESSENTIALS REQUIRED OF TUTORS

◆ Tutors need to have an excellent knowledge of their subject and be able to pass this on to their pupils. Not all classroom teachers would be suitable for one-to-one tutoring which requires different skills. Many graduates will make good tutors even though they have never taught in a classroom. They need to have a love of their subject, which they can communicate enthusiastically to their pupils.

◆ Tutors need to be punctual and reliable. Clients will lose confidence in tutors who are constantly late or who often change the dates of lessons.

◆ Tutors should be appropriately dressed and behave in a professional manner which will not distract or alarm a pupil. For example, they should not smoke or use a mobile telephone during lessons.

◆ Tutors must have a good command of the English language as well as good communication skills. This will become clear when they ring in response to the recruitment advertisement.

◆ Tutors will be expected by clients to arrive at lessons well prepared and to have a good supply of teaching materials.

◆ Tutors must be honest and trustworthy. Clients have to feel confident enough to leave their children alone with a tutor. The agency needs to trust that tutors will pay the correct amount of commission and will not make private arrangements with clients who have been introduced to them through the agency.

◆ Tutors need to provide the agency with a full CV, two references, a fully completed application form, a disclaimer form and, if possible, a copy of their CRB disclosure (see Chapter 3).

◆ Tutors need to be able to adapt to their students' individual needs and to establish a good rapport with them. Pupils will respond well if the subject is taught in a lively and interesting manner and if they are stimulated but not stressed.

◆ Tutors should be able to assess pupils' abilities and pitch lessons at the right level, whether they are preparing a pupil for Oxbridge entrance or helping them progress from a D to a C at A-level.

◆ Tutors need to give parents and pupils realistic expectations while not diminishing a child's confidence.

◆ Tutors who teach in their own homes need to set aside a suitable area in their house where pupils will feel comfortable and secure. There should be a clearly defined teaching space with two chairs and an uncluttered writing surface. Tutors must ensure that there are no interruptions to lessons. It would be unprofessional for a tutor to take or make telephone calls or deal with family matters during the course of a lesson.

14

CASE STUDIES

CASE STUDY 1

Mrs Ray rang the agency following a parents' evening in early November at her son's primary school. Bhavik is in Year 2 and has not yet grasped the essentials of numeracy and literacy. His teacher was concerned that he had, over the past few weeks, become slightly withdrawn and was not as attentive as he had been at the beginning of term. His mother reported back to the teacher that she had trouble getting him to go to school and he was often tearful on his way to and from school.

We suggested that Bhavik would benefit from one-to-one tuition to restore his confidence and enthusiasm. Mrs Ray was concerned about the cost of tuition and assumed that she would be locked into a long-term arrangement with the agency. We assured her that at Bhavik's age he would progress quickly over a short period of individual tuition.

Tuition started in mid-November and continued until February half-term when Mrs Ray reported back to the agency that Bhavik had come on in leaps and bounds and was now a happy, settled little boy who was doing well in class.

CASE STUDY 2

Alexander rang the agency on a Friday evening in January. He was in the Upper Sixth at a local sixth-form college and had an exam in Chemistry on Monday morning. Whilst revising that week he had realised that he was having problems understanding one topic of the course. He was desperate for some help and had contacted several other local tutoring agencies who had all said that it was too late in the day to do anything for him. We contacted an experienced A-level chemistry tutor who booked two two-hour lessons with Alexander over that weekend.

Following his exam, Alexander went on to book weekly lessons with the same tutor until his last exam in June, and we later learnt from the tutor that Alexander had gained an A in his A-level Chemistry exam.

CASE STUDY 3

Mrs Roberts contacted the agency in May. Her ten-year-old daughter Zoe attended her local primary school where she was top of her class. Mrs Roberts was keen for her daughter to sit an entrance exam for a local grammar school. While Zoe was doing extremely well in school, she was not being prepared for a timed exam situation and she had never had an opportunity to see the sort of exam papers that she would face.

We allocated Zoe a tutor who specialised in entrance exam preparation, who tutored her until the examination in January. Mrs Roberts was delighted when Zoe was offered a place at their chosen school.

CASE STUDY 4

Oliver Thompson had been bullied at school and his parents had removed him from the school and were awaiting a place for him elsewhere. He was in Year 9 at secondary school and initially his mother asked the agency to provide tutors in the nine subjects that he had been studying in class.

Mrs Thompson was advised by the agency that it was important for Oliver to concentrate on the subjects which would be most valuable in preparing him for the GCSE syllabus. He needed to keep up with Maths, Science, English and Spanish, but it would not matter if he missed some History, Geography, IT, and Art.

We set Oliver up with a tutor who taught Maths and Science and

another who taught English and Spanish. Mrs Thompson heard from
the local education authority that it would take at least ten weeks to find
Oliver a new school. At this point the agency negotiated a ten-week
financial package between Mrs Thompson and the tutors. This offered
her a discount when she booked for a total of eight hours' tuition per
week which she paid for in advance.

15

BECOMING A HOME TUTOR

'Tell me and I'll forget; show me and I may remember; involve me and I'll understand.'
CHINESE PROVERB

This chapter is designed to help you get started as a home tutor. The first part of the chapter is aimed at qualified teachers. The second part is aimed at graduates who wish to set themselves up as home tutors but who have little or no previous teaching experience.

QUALITIES OF A HOME TUTOR

There are certain qualities required of all home tutors. These include the following:

◆ Having an excellent knowledge and love of their subject.
◆ Being punctual and reliable.
◆ Behaving in a professional manner.
◆ Having a good command of the English language.
◆ Being well prepared, with a good supply of teaching materials.
◆ Being able to assess a pupil's individual needs.
◆ Having realistic expectations of a student's ability.

For a fuller explanation of these qualities, see Chapter 13 (page 74).

QUALIFIED TEACHERS

Why

1. To supplement your teaching income.
2. To keep your hand in following your recent retirement from teaching.

3. To earn some money whilst taking time out from teaching.

How

1. If you have been teaching for some time in your local area and have a proven track record as a good teacher you will probably find that you already know pupils who would like you to give them some private lessons.

2. The pupils you tutor will then recommend you to others.

3. You may need to boost your supply of pupils by occasionally putting an advertisement in your local newspaper, but this is expensive. (Most libraries will not take advertisements from individual tutors.)

4. You may wish to join a tutoring agency. Although you will pay some of your income back to the agency in commission, they will supply you with pupils, do all the associated administration, set the rates, deal with awkward clients and save you money on advertising.

Where to tutor

1. **In your own home**. Set aside a suitable area in your house where pupils will feel comfortable and secure. There should be a clearly defined teaching space with two chairs and an uncluttered writing surface. Ensure that there are no interruptions to lessons. It would be unprofessional to make or take telephone calls or to deal with family matters during the course of a lesson.

2. **In the pupil's home**. Before the first lesson you need to ensure that parents can provide a suitable, comfortable, quiet area in the house in which the lesson can take place without interruption. You should arrive punctually and be well prepared for every lesson.

No matter where you teach, make sure that lessons start and finish on time. Do not allow lessons to overrun by more than five to ten minutes. A brief discussion with parents about a child's progress at the end of a lesson is acceptable but should they require an in-depth discussion make it clear that you need to charge for your time.

What do you need?

1. A good supply of recent resources (see Chapter 11). You may have supplies of books and papers of your own, but remember that they don't stay current for long.

2. Stay in touch with colleagues who are still teaching in order to keep up to date with all the changes to the curriculum.

3. Keep copies of your references and your CRB disclosure form as you may be asked by parents or a tutoring agency to provide these.

PAYMENT

1. If you are working independently you need to set your rates at the same level as those of other local tutors.

2. Make sure that you are paid at the end of every lesson taught.

3. You need to keep an accurate account of your earnings and expenses for tax purposes.

GRADUATES

Why

1. To supplement their income.

2. To gain experience whilst considering a career in teaching.

3. To finance a further degree or qualification.

How

1. Join a tutoring agency because it is a good idea for those who do not have teaching experience. A good agency will support you in taking the first steps towards becoming a home tutor. They will also recommend resources, put you in touch with experienced tutors for their advice, provide you with pupils and give you ongoing support.

2. Put an advertisement in the local newspaper. However, this is expensive because you will need to advertise for several weeks in order to attract enough pupils. These days, for reasons of safety, parents are less likely to pick out an individual's name from the

newspaper, preferring to use the services of a tutoring agency who vet their tutors.

Where

1. **In your own home**. Set aside a suitable area in your house where pupils will feel comfortable and secure. There should be a clearly defined teaching space with two chairs and an uncluttered writing surface. Ensure that there are no interruptions to lessons. It would be unprofessional to make or take telephone calls or to deal with family matters during the course of a lesson.

2. **In the pupil's home**. Before the first lesson you need to ensure that parents can provide a suitable, comfortable, quiet area in the house in which the lesson can take place without interruption. You should arrive punctually and be well prepared for every lesson.

No matter where you teach, make sure that lessons start and finish on time. Do not allow lessons to overrun by more than five to ten minutes. A brief discussion with parents about a child's progress at the end of a lesson is acceptable but should they require an in depth discussion make it clear that you need to charge for your time.

THE NATIONAL CURRICULUM

Parents are immediately aware if tutors are not competent and confident. You need to research thoroughly the syllabus of the subject you wish to teach and familiarise yourself with the National Curriculum. The National Curriculum sets out the stages and core subjects which children will be taught throughout their school lives. Children aged five to 16 in state or maintained schools must be taught according to the National Curriculum. The National Curriculum is a framework used by all maintained schools to ensure that teaching and learning is balanced and consistent.

It sets out:

♦ the subjects taught;

- the knowledge, skills and understanding required in each subject;
- standards or attainment targets in each subject that teachers can use to measure children's progress and plan their future learning;
- how children's progress is assessed and reported.

Within the framework of the National Curriculum schools are free to plan and organise teaching and learning in the way that best meets the needs of their pupils. Many schools use the Qualifications and Curriculum Authority (QCA) Schemes of Work to plan the curriculum. These provide a basis for delivering the National Curriculum. For more information on the National Curriculum see www.direct.gov.uk

THE NATIONAL EXAMINATION SYSTEM

Be familiar with the national examination system:

School entrance exams at the ages of 7, 11 and 13 years. For entrance to selective schools there will be exams in maths, English, verbal and non-verbal reasoning and possibly science. Sample or past exam papers may be available from the individual school. You will need to contact the school to see if they will sell you some papers or it may be possible to download papers from the school's website.

SATs (Standard Attainment Tests) are taken at the ages of 7, 11 and 14 years. The National Curriculum divides these into Key Stages 1, 2, and 3. The tests at these Key Stages show children's performances in selected parts of a subject on a particular day. For example, at the end of Key Stage 2 pupils are tested in English, Maths and Science. These tests give an independent measure of how pupils and schools are doing compared with national standards in these subjects. For further information on SATs see www.sats-past-papers.co.uk

GCSEs and A-levels. As well as having a good course book you will need to contact the appropriate examination board to purchase a syllabus, past papers, marking schemes and examiners' reports. An examiner's report will show you the best work achieved and the most commonly made mistakes. The names and contact details of all examination boards are provided in Chapter 11.

Build up a supply of resources from a good bookshop, a local library, the internet or from friends who may be teachers (see Chapter 11).

You will need to have two up-to-date references and possibly a CRB disclosure.

PAYMENT

1. If you are working independently you need to set your rates at the same level as those of other local tutors.

2. Make sure that you are paid at the end of every lesson taught.

3. You need to keep an accurate account of your earnings and expenses for tax purposes.

Part II
STARTING YOUR OWN BUSINESS —
USEFUL INFORMATION

16

TAX AND NATIONAL INSURANCE FOR THE SELF-EMPLOYED

If you have always been an employee your income tax and national insurance will have been deducted at source. As a self-employed person you will be responsible for paying your own income tax and national insurance.

INCOME TAX

If you are newly self-employed you need to notify HM Revenue and Customs. You can do this by calling their helpline number 08459 154515. This alerts them that you will be sending in a tax return at the end of the financial year for your new business.

It is very important to keep an accurate and detailed record of your business earnings and expenditure so that you can calculate your taxable profit at the end of the tax year. Records of expenditure should include details of major purchases such as a computer or telephone system, as well as the day-to-day running costs such as stationery or postage. It is a legal requirement to keep all accounting records for five years.

The tax year runs from 6 April to the following 5 April. You may decide to use the services of a bookkeeper or an accountant to fill in your tax return. Alternatively you may wish to do your own accounting in which case you need to fill in your tax return giving details of taxable income and claiming any allowance. This means that you are responsible for ensuring that you pay the right amount of tax. Your tax return can be filled in either on paper or on line. There are excellent guides to help you to complete the form.

Once the form is completed you then need to decide whether you want to calculate the tax or whether you want HM Revenue and Customs to do this. You should bear in mind that if you want HM Revenue and Customs to calculate your tax for you, the completed form has to be sent in by 30 September following the end of the tax year. The final date for sending in all completed tax returns is 31 January following the end of the tax year. You will be fined if you do not send your tax return in on time.

HM Revenue and Customs will send you a bill shortly before you need to pay your tax. Tax is usually paid in two instalments, 31 January and 31 July. Late payment of tax incurs interest charges.

For further information on income tax for the self employed visit www.hmrc.gov.uk

NATIONAL INSURANCE CONTRIBUTIONS

National Insurance (NI) is a tax paid from wages to finance state benefits such as sickness, unemployment and retirement pensions. As a self-employed person you will be responsible for paying your own NI contributions. The amount payable depends on the amount you earn. Class 1 NI is for employees and Class 2 NI is for the self-employed. If you are starting up your tutoring agency while you are still an employee, you will need to pay both Class 1 and Class 2 NI. The current rate of Class 2 NI is £2.20 per week. HM Revenue and Customs collect NI and they send you a bill every three months. For further detailed information visit www.hmrc.gov.uk or contact:

HM Revenue and Customs
National Insurance Contributions Office
Self Employment Services
Longbenton
Newcastle upon Tyne
NE98 1ZZ

Or call the self employed contact centre on 0845 915 4655.

BENEFITS AND TAX CREDITS

If you are self-employed and on a low income you may be entitled to claim benefits or tax credits. For more information and help contact your local Citizens Advice Bureau.

VALUE ADDED TAX (VAT)

VAT is a tax that you pay when you buy goods and services. A business with an annual turnover of less than £61,000 does not need to register for or pay VAT. Should you need further information on this tax contact HM Revenue and Customs (HMRC) national advice service on 0845 010 9000.

17

PENSIONS

The basic state pension is a government-administered pension, based on the number of qualifying years gained through paying National Insurance contributions. As a self-employed person paying Class 2 National Insurance contributions (see Chapter 16) you will be entitled to a State Pension. You become entitled to a State Pension when you reach the age of 65 (men) and 60 (women).

In addition, you may wish to save for your retirement by investing in a private pension. It is well worthwhile seeking independent expert advice on the various options available.

PERSONAL PENSION PLANS (PPPs)

PPPs are investment policies for retirement which offer a lump sum and an income in retirement between the ages of 50 and 75 years. You can purchase a PPP from an insurance company, a high street bank, an investment company or some retailers. The money that you contribute to your PPP is invested for you, a fund is built up and then the lump sum and income become available to you when you choose to retire. The amount of pension payable upon retirement depends on:

- The amount of money which has been paid into the scheme.

- The performance of the investment funds.

- The annuity rate at the date of retirement. (An annuity rate is the factor used to convert the amount invested into a pension.)

STAKEHOLDER PENSION SCHEMES

This is a type of PPP. The Stakeholder Pension Schemes, like the PPP, provide a lump sum and an income on retirement. They can be purchased from the same providers as a PPP. A Stakeholder Pension Scheme incorporates minimum standards laid down by the government. These include:

◆ A charging structure capped at 1.5% of the fund each year for the first ten years and 1% per year thereafter.

◆ No penalties on increasing, decreasing, stopping and restarting contributions.

◆ No penalties on transferring the fund to another pension arrangement.

◆ A minimum contribution of £20.

SELF-INVESTED PERSONAL PENSIONS (SIPP)

These are similar to PPPs as far as contributions and eligibility are concerned. However, whereas with a PPP your premium is invested for you and you have little choice about the investment, with an SIPP you have greater control over the investment, or you can appoint a fund manager or stockbroker to manage your investments for you.

For further help and advice contact:

Financial Services Authority: Offers general information about financial services and products. Phone 0845 606 1234 or visit www.moneymaker.
fsa.gov.uk

Independent financial advisers: You can also contact an independent financial adviser, but remember, you will generally have to pay for this.

The Pensions Advisory Service: For free information and guidance about company, personal or stakeholder pensions, phone The Pensions Advisory Service on 0845 601 2923 or visit www.pensionsadvisory service.org.uk

18
HOW TO TRADE

Once you have decided to start your own home tutoring agency you need to consider the different ways in which your business can be set up. There are three possibilities that are suitable for this type of business.

SOLE TRADER

The simplest, cheapest and by far the most popular way to set up your tutoring agency is as a sole trader. The advantages of being a sole trader are:

◆ You are entitled to all the profits of the business.

◆ All allowable expenses of the business can be offset against income tax. For income tax and National Insurance contributions and for advice on informing the necessary government agencies that you are starting a business see Chapter 16.

◆ You do not have to register with Companies House.

◆ You make your own decisions and have complete control of the business.

◆ You can pass the business on to a member of your family when you retire.

PARTNERSHIPS

Setting up your tutoring agency as a partnership is a convenient way for two or more people running a business together. Choose your partner(s) carefully. You do not need to have a written partnership agreement. However, if you wish to make this arrangement more formal then a simple written, signed partnership agreement is advisable.

An ideal partner would be someone who:

* you know well;
* you trust;
* is equally enthusiastic about starting a tutoring agency;
* you know you can work well with;
* is geographically close to you;
* has expertise which complements yours;
* is able to devote an equal amount of time to the business as you;
* is able to share the initial costs of setting up the business.

The advantages of partnerships are:

* you share the workload;
* you share the costs;
* you share the good times and the bad;
* there is a greater fund of expertise, talents and ideas;
* there is a cover for the business when one partner wants time out.

LIMITED COMPANY

Setting up your business as a limited company is more complicated and expensive than setting it up as a sole trader or partnership and because of this it would be advisable to use the services of an accountant.

To set up a limited company you need to:

* contact Companies House which will supply you with an information pack about how to register your company and the fee involved;
* appoint a company secretary;
* choose a name for your business and ask Companies House to check its availability.

The obligations of a limited company include:

* Annual accounts must be prepared and submitted to Companies House.
* An annual return must be completed and sent to Companies House.

This return details key company facts and personnel.

- Annual accounts and annual returns incur a small fee and there are financial penalties if they are not sent to Companies House on time.
- Payment of corporation tax.

Advantages of a limited company:

- Limitation of personal liability.
- Bank loans are more easily obtainable because of the lower level of liability.
- It affords greater status in the business world.
- Provides a stronger platform for growth.

For further information on limited companies visit www.companies house.gov.uk

19

FURNISHING AND EQUIPPING YOUR HOME OFFICE

Working from home has many advantages and helps to keep running costs low. You can use any corner of your home, it is not necessary to have a high tech office. As your tutoring agency builds up you may want to spend some money on setting up a specific area within your home and on up-to-date equipment which will make your business more efficient.

WHY HAVE YOUR OFFICE AT HOME?

◆ All you need to start your business is a pen, paper and a telephone.

◆ It cuts out the need to find premises and the necessity of having to apply for permission to change the use of premises, i.e. from a shop to an office.

◆ It avoids the large expenses of rent, rates, insurance, solicitor's costs, etc.

◆ You can offset some home costs such as heating, wear and tear, electricity and telephone bills against income tax.

◆ There are no travelling expenses and no time is wasted getting to and from work.

◆ You will enjoy flexible working hours.

◆ Your time can be efficiently used, for example during a quiet period in the day, you can get on with the business of your household.

◆ You may have ready made staff on hand. Partners, grown up children, flatmates, etc., can all be taught to answer the telephone for you if necessary.

- You do not need to pay business rates to carry on this business in your home.

WHERE YOU CAN WORK IN YOUR HOME

- In reality you do not need any designated workspace to run a home tutoring agency. All you need is to have your telephone, notepad and pen handy.

- If you are lucky enough to have a spare room in your home then part or all of it could be used as your designated office.

- You can also consider utilising spare attic or loft space as an office.

- If you have a noisy household you may prefer to convert a part of a garage or a garden shed to provide office space.

EQUIPMENT AND FURNITURE

- In the beginning all you need is a telephone, notepad, pen, two card-index boxes (one for tutors and one for clients) and a notebook in which to keep records of your income and expenditure.

- Initially you can use your home telephone number. However, as business increases, you may find that it is useful to have a dedicated business line.

- An answering machine or an answerphone service will ensure that you never miss a business call.

- If you are away from home for lengthy periods, you may choose to set up a call transfer service to a mobile telephone.

- Once your business is flourishing you may wish to buy a desk and a comfortable chair, shelving or a small filing cabinet for stationery.

- A desk-top computer and printer will make a busy business more time- and energy-efficient.

- A laptop computer will make your tutoring agency even more portable.

20

GOING ON TO BIGGER THINGS

Once your tutoring agency is flourishing you can consider trying out new ideas which will increase your earning potential. As mentioned in Chapter 10 you can do this by providing special courses or by moving into the business of supply teaching. These additions are not too time consuming and will not change the nature of your core business but will add to its breadth and provide more income. If, however, you are looking for a more exciting and challenging way of expanding your tutoring agency business you may wish to consider the following options.

WIDENING YOUR EXISTING GEOGRAPHICAL AREA

If you have started your tutoring agency in Edgstone E12, Carlton E20 and Stanbridge E10 for example, you may wish to consider including three other local areas so that the total area covered by your business doubles. This does not change the basic nature of the business but does give it greater potential. It is likely that you are almost as familiar with your new areas as you are with your existing ones. You can continue with this type of expansion until you feel your business is as large as you can manage or you may wish to look at the next option.

A NEW GEOGRAPHICAL AREA

You can start another tutoring agency in an entirely new geographical area to run alongside your existing one. You already have in place all the skills you need for this new venture which could double your income.

However, if you find that this stretches you too far, you could consider employing a manager. It would be an advantage if that person lived within the new area as they will be familiar with its local schools, newspapers, etc. This involves becoming an employer with all the responsibilities that this entails. For further information see www.businesslink.gov.uk

BUYING OUT A COMPETITOR

An opportunity may arise for you to purchase an existing local tutoring agency which could be added to your business. Buying a ready-made business has three main advantages:

+ it eliminates a local competitor;
+ it adds an established database of tutors to your own thus saving the cost of advertising for more tutors;
+ it increases your income by taking over all their current clients.

FRANCHISING

Once your business is running successfully and you would like to take a giant leap in expanding it, franchising could be an exciting and interesting way forward for you.

What is a franchise?

A franchise is an agreement between a service provider (the franchisor) and a person who wishes to use that service provider's name and expertise according to a given pattern of business (the franchisee). This offers the franchisee assistance in organising, training, marketing and managing in return for an initial fee plus an ongoing percentage of profits.

This form of expansion has a proven, successful track record with many well known brands, now household names, for example, McDonald's, Kall-Kwik, The Body Shop and Starbucks.

Franchising is for those who are ambitious and want a business which, while being extremely time consuming, could offer enormous rewards.

Your tutoring agency business is suitable for franchising because:

- It has a proven, unique, successful formula with a good track record.

- You have the necessary expertise to help others set up their own tutoring agency and to offer ongoing support.

- It is making enough money to attract franchisees.

- The formula, procedures, expertise and skills are transferable to others who can be trained in a short amount of time.

- You have the knowledge to gauge the correct price for the purchase of a franchise. You can strike the right balance between making a good profit while at the same time making it attractive and affordable to franchisees.

You will need to bear in mind that:

- You need to use the services of a franchise consultant, accountants and solicitors.

- There are costs involved in setting up a franchise.

- While you own the franchised business you do not control the day-to-day running of it.

- Franchises have to be monitored closely and you need support staff to help you do this.

- You need to invest time in recruiting the right franchisees.

- There can be conflicts between franchisors and franchisees.

For further information see www.whichfranchise.com

21

SETTING UP A WEBSITE

Whilst the majority of your tutors and clients will find you via the local paper others will use the internet as a channel for information. You may therefore wish to consider having a website. Have a look at your competitors' websites, making a note of what you like and dislike about them.

CREATING A WEBSITE

Unless you have the expertise to set up your own website it would be well worth investing in the services of a web design consultant. They will set up your website for you based on the information you give them about your business and what you want your website to achieve.

ADVANTAGES OF HAVING A WEBSITE

- It is an excellent marketing tool for your business.

- It reaches a wide audience.

- It is available at all times.

- You can update it as often as you want.

- You can give much more information than you can in a newspaper advertisement.

- It raises your company profile.

- The costs of maintaining your site are low compared with other media.

COSTS

It is difficult to be precise about the cost of building a website. Setting up a basic site can cost as little as £300 while a more sophisticated site could cost thousands of pounds.

The cost of setting up a basic website which will suit a tutoring agency business should include:

◆ The services of a web design consultant.

◆ The creation of one or two web pages.

◆ Registration of domain name and web hosting for 12 months.

◆ One email address.

◆ If you want to use a statistics service showing the number of visitors this will cost an extra £30 p.a.

◆ If you register your website on a search engine you will need to pay for this service.

MAKING YOUR WEBSITE KNOWN

There are various ways in which people will find your website:

◆ You can add your website address to all your stationery.

◆ You can add your website address to all advertisements.

◆ You can pay to have your website registered on a search engine such as Google. For further information on search engines see www.search enginewatch.com

22

FINANCIAL HELP FOR SMALL BUSINESSES

A unique feature of a tutoring agency business is that it needs a minimal amount of money to get it off the ground. Assuming that you have a telephone, a notepad and a pen, the only initial outlay is on advertising. You need to start with a four to six week period of advertising to recruit your tutors which will cost as little as £400. Thereafter you would only place a tutor recruitment advertisement for one week, two or three times per year.

Once your tutors have been recruited you can begin to advertise for clients. These advertisements cost approximately £40 per week. You will start earning money as soon as you begin advertising for clients.

HOW TO FINANCE YOUR INITIAL ADVERTISING CAMPAIGN

There are several options.

* The least expensive money to use for your enterprise is your own because it comes without interest charges. The initial expenditure is so small that it is worth dipping into savings.

* If you are still in full- or part-time work you may choose to use some of your income to finance your start-up costs. Remember these will be spread over a period of several weeks and advertising bills are paid retrospectively.

* You could try asking friends or relations for some initial financial help before turning to organisations which charge interest.

* A bank overdraft is ideal for short-term borrowing.

* You could negotiate a bank loan.

ONGOING FINANCE

If you have decided to give up work to start your tutoring agency and need to borrow a larger amount of money to finance several months of living expenses until your business takes off, or if you wish to spend money on buying equipment such as a computer there are other options open to you.

GRANTS

Grants are a wonderful idea because generally you do not have to pay them back. Here are some useful contacts.

◆ To help you look for the appropriate grant go to www.j4b.co.uk which is a grant finding service.

◆ Contact your local Business Link which has been set up by the government to provide a free consultation service for small businesses: www.businesslink.gov.uk

◆ You may be eligible to apply for a grant from the Department of Trade and Industry (DTI): www.dti.gov.uk

◆ If you are between the ages of 18 and 30 you may be eligible for a grant from the Prince's Trust: www.princes-trust.org.uk

LOANS

Loans come in many shapes and sizes but generally need to be repaid. Here are some suggestions:

◆ Soft loans are unsecured and generally available to those who cannot get a bank loan. They are usually offered at a reduced interest rate and are available from local authorities, Local Enterprise Trusts, Training and Enterprise Councils (TEC) and Local Enterprise Councils (LEC).

◆ Some high street banks offer special small business start-up loans.

◆ Small Firms Loan Guarantee Scheme from the DTI: www.dti.gov.uk

DO REMEMBER

♦ When running a business from home it is possible to offset some of your household expenses against income tax, e.g. electricity and telephone bills.

♦ Everything you spend in connection with the business can be offset against income tax, e.g. postage, stationery and equipment.

♦ Personal pension scheme payments are partially tax deductible.

USEFUL ADDRESSES AND WEBSITES

Times Educational Supplement (TES)
www.tes.co.uk
Tel: 020 7782 3000

Criminal Records Bureau (CRB)
www.crb.gov.uk
Tel: 0870 909 0811

Assessment and Qualifications Alliance (AQA North)
Devas Street
Manchester
M15 6EX
Tel: 0161 953 1180
Fax: 0161 455 5444
www.aqa.org.uk

Assessment and Qualifications Alliance (AQA South)
Stag Hill House
Guildford
Surrey
GU2 5XJ
Tel: 01483 506 506
Fax: 01483 300 152
www.aqa.org.uk

City & Guilds
1 Giltspur Street
London
EC1A 9DD
Tel: 020 7294 2800

Fax: 020 7294 2400

www.city-and-guilds.co.uk

Edexcel

190 High Holborn

London

WC1V 7BH

Tel: 0870 240 9800

Fax: 020 7190 5700

Minicom: 0870 240 3941

www.edexcel.org.uk

Northern Ireland Council for the Curriculum

Examinations and Assessment (CCEA)

29 Clarendon Road

Belfast

BT1 3BG

Tel: 02890 261 200

Fax: 02890 261 234

www.ccea.org.uk

Oxford, Cambridge and RSA (OCR)

Syndicate Buildings

1 Hills Road

Cambridge

CB1 2EU

Tel: 01223 553 998

Fax: 01223 552 627

www.ocr.org.uk

Scottish Qualifications Authority (SQA)

Hanover House

24 Douglas Street

Glasgow

G2 7NQ

Tel: 0845 279 1000

Fax: 0141-242 2244

www.sqa.org.uk

Welsh Joint Education Committee

245 Western Avenue

Cardiff

CF5 2YX

Tel: 02920 265 000 (main switchboard) or 02920 265 155 (GCSE administration)

www.wjec.co.uk

Joint Council for Qualifications (JCQ)

Veritas House

125 Finsbury Pavement

London

EC2A 1NQ

www.jcq.org.uk

International Baccalaureate Organization

Peterson House

Malthouse Avenue

Cardiff Gate

Cardiff

CF23 8GL

Tel: 0292 0547 777

Fax: 0292 0547 778

www.ibo.org

Independent Schools Examinations Board (ISEB)

Jordan House

Christchurch Road

New Milton

BH25 6QJ

Tel: 01425 621111

Fax: 01425 620044

www.iseb.co.uk

National Curriculum
www.direct.gov.uk

HM Revenue and Customs
Helpline: 08459 154515.
www.hmrc.gov.uk

HM Revenue and Customs
National Insurance Contributions Office
Self Employment Services
Longbenton
Newcastle upon Tyne
NE98 1ZZ
Self employed contact centre. Tel: 0845 915 4655

HM Revenues and Customs (HMRC) National Advice Service
Tel: 0845 010 9000.

Financial Services Authority
Offers general information about financial services and products.
Tel: 0845 606 1234
www.moneymaker.fsa.gov.uk

Independent Financial Advisers
You can also contact an independent financial adviser, but remember, you will generally have to pay for this.

The Pensions Advisory Service
For free information and guidance about company, personal or stakeholder pensions:
Tel: 0845 601 2923
www.pensionsadvisoryservice.org.uk

Companies House
www.companieshouse.gov.uk

For information on franchising
www.whichfranchise.com

For information on search engines
www.searchenginewatch.com

For information on grants:
www.j4b.co.uk
www.businesslink.gov.uk
www.dti.gov.uk
www.princes-trust.org.uk

**For further information or consultation email:
torringtontutors@hotmail.co.uk**

FINAL NOTE

'It is never too late to be what you might have been.'

GEORGE ELIOT

Now that you have read the book, you are one step away from an enjoyable career which will provide you with a good income, a flexible lifestyle and an exciting new challenge. Take the plunge, you will not regret it. Good luck.

For further information or consultation email:
torringtontutors@hotmail.co.uk

INDEX